lead.

lead.

KARL MARTIN

First published in 2017 by
Muddy Pearl, Edinburgh, Scotland.
www.muddypearl.com
books@muddypearl.com

British Library Cataloguing in Publication Data
A catalogue record for this book is available from the British Library

ISBN 978-1-910012-15-4

Typeset in Minion by Waverley Typesetters, Warham, Norfolk
Printed in Great Britain by Bell & Bain Ltd, Glasgow

To my family, immediate and extended.
N L K A E: you are my team.
E&K and G&A: you have lived this with us.
To all those I have had the privilege to lead, especially my teams at Central and Cairn:
thank you for your courage, your faith in God and your trust in me. You have made it all worth it. I am the richest of leaders because of the teams I lead.

Contents

Foreword

It is honoring and intimidating when someone asks you to write a foreword for their book. Giving a foreword to my good friend Karl himself would have been much easier. Yet what I know of Karl completely qualifies him to write about leadership. In this book are principles and material that will help leaders of all ages and at all stages of their leadership journey. Digesting it will be well worth your time, and if you are fortunate enough to get this material in your twenties, you are the better for it.

There are two qualities that every great leader possesses: *availability* and *teachability*. Availability is an attitude that reflects what the great prophet Isaiah said: 'Here I am, Lord. Send me!' One of the most consistent prayers I pray is, 'God, if you have anything going on today, I want to be a part of it. I'm available.'

Teachability is the aptitude of receiving and applying new information. Too many leaders want others to take their ideas and their teachings without ever stretching to receive and apply information from others. God often teaches us through his people. Halfway through this book Karl tells a story of his teachability that I remember well. It is the kind of event that qualifies him to be a leader worthy of writing this book.

We never stop developing as leaders, but the steeper your growth curve in the early years of your leadership journey the more joyful and impactful your life will be. An early mentor of mine said, 'The greatest work God is doing is the work in you.'

As a younger leader I didn't believe that. I was all about the event, the organisation, the numbers, the notoriety, or the hill to be conquered. I was surprised by how turning 40 was a bit traumatic. It wasn't that I felt older. It was that I *was* older. Life was starting to speed by with increasing intensity. Turning 40 meant that I could no longer bear the title of 'young leader' and enjoy all the benefits of that moniker.

Young leaders are expected to make mistakes. Young leaders get extra grace from others as they stumble through leadership situations. Young leaders also know that their best days are ahead of them. At 40 I realised, 'I'm no longer a young leader. My mistakes now have big consequences and my best days are here. Am I leveraging my life appropriately?'

When I turned 50, it marked the realisation that not only was I *not* an up and coming leader but I needed to start thinking about my endgame. If old age comes on me half as fast as middle age did, by tomorrow I'll be watching afternoon television while gumming my cream of wheat for lunch. Age has brought me more awareness of what matters and how to get it done.

There is a place for ambition. Not the unhealthy kind that Karl warns against, but the kind that springs from a leader who wants to be used. A leader who wants to be on the front lines. A leader who longs to look at their life and know that they mattered. This isn't narcissism. This is the great commission. This book will teach available leaders how to partner with the work of God regardless of what leg of the race you are on.

BRIAN TOME
Cincinatti
November 2016

STAKE

The function of leadership is to produce more leaders, not more followers.

Ralph Nader

•

As Jesus was walking beside the Sea of Galilee, he saw two brothers, Simon called Peter and his brother Andrew. They were casting a net into the lake, for they were fishermen. 'Come, follow me,' Jesus said, 'and I will send you out to fish for people.' At once they left their nets and followed him.

Going on from there, he saw two other brothers, James son of Zebedee and his brother John. They were in a boat with their father Zebedee, preparing their nets. Jesus called them, and immediately they left the boat and their father and followed him.

Matthew 4:18–22

Then Jesus came to them and said, 'All authority in heaven and on earth has been given to me. Therefore go and make disciples of all nations, baptising them in the name of the Father and of the Son and of the Holy Spirit, and teaching them to obey everything I have commanded you. And surely I am with you always, to the very end of the age.'

Matthew 28:18–20

Read this book responsibly.

I am of course aware that starting a book on leadership with the kind of phrase usually reserved for the label of a bottle of whisky or a packet of fireworks is dangerous, even arrogant. But what I mean to do is to deflect the reader from the natural thought,

'This is not for me.
Not about me.
Not applicable to me.'

My desire is to encourage you, and me, in the taking of responsibility – for the leadership we do have, and also in reaching for the leadership we might have. To be the leader and to do the tasks of leadership to the very best of our God-given abilities. It is just not going to work for me to say, 'This is not for me.' I became a leader the very moment I was born. So did you. You began to lead yourself, and ultimately influence others. Christian, the moment you were born again, the moment you said 'Yes' to following Jesus, that leadership just grew, it multiplied, you not only became a disciple, you became a disciple maker. A disciple that makes disciples that make disciples. That's what you signed up for.

You are a leader, settle that now.

And read this book responsibly.

The Apostle Paul, when writing to the church at Philippi implores his readers to take hold of that for which Christ has taken hold of you.

Read this book responsibly. It is said by Luke that the first disciples devoted themselves. They devoted themselves to prayer, to the apostles teaching, to breaking bread (Acts 2:42) – with a sense of continuing, persevering, applying something. See, there is a leadership quality that is rarely spoken of and yet underpins all great leadership.

Responsibility.

'It's on me.'

The first disciples, the first leaders of this beautiful family that changed the world, devoted themselves. They took responsibility for their call and for their leadership. They did so because of what they had seen and heard, at the feet of, and on the road with, the greatest leader who ever lived.

Read this book responsibly.

Now, trace a circle, draw a line, plant a stake.

That's the way I introduce leadership to any new group of interns. It is a call to responsibility, to devotion. To the leadership of yourself, and others. And it is so important.

It is on this wonderful heavenly gift called leadership, that everything on this earth stands or falls. I believe that God is always speaking over us and equipping us with the tools and energy to take responsibility to deal with our stuff and to run with our dreams.

To trace a circle, to draw a line, to plant a stake.

It's what he was doing with Moses, at a bush, by the sea, and on a mountain. It's what he was doing with Elijah and Joshua and all the guys mentioned in Hebrews Chapter 11. It's what he does with Peter and Paul and the other apprentice disciples. He is drawing us into leadership. He is trying to grow big people. To take big responsibility. To run with big dreams.

The way of the circle, and the line and the stake will start to grow you and those around you.

My call to leadership came in a bath. After a football match. I had just scored the winning goal in the University Championships and I was having a reflective moment on my own. (Pretty rare for me, I'm an extreme extrovert.) I wasn't really following Jesus at the time. I was thinking about last night's conversation with my three closest friends. None of them knew Jesus: one was a nominal Christian, one an atheistic Jew, and the third a lover of hip-hop and eccentric fashion. They joked with me: 'What we love about you Karl, is that you'd call yourself a Christian, but we would never know it by the way you live.' They meant it as a compliment. Those words cut me to the heart.

In the bath I did a deal with God, 'Show me this stuff is real, or I'm all out. No more guilt, shame, rules, or limits. I'm totally out.'

I'm not sure the bath is the best place for this conversation. I was completely exposed. But God showed up. There were no bolts of lightning but there was an arresting presence that could not be denied. I knew that God was in the room with me. I knew that all I had half-believed, was true.

'All out' became 'all in'.

I knew that every gift, ability and power that I had, came from him and was to be used for him. That began my call. The where, with whom, what and when was all for later, but I knew my life was his, my abilities were his, my future was his.

When God wants something done he looks for a leader. Check it out. Throughout the Scriptures, throughout church history, he looks for a leader of character, a leader after his own heart, a leader who lives beyond themselves. Sometimes an unlikely leader. But he is always looking for a leader. When God wants the Midianites defeated he raises up Gideon. When he wants to free his people from slavery he raises up Moses. When he wants to save his people from destruction he calls Esther. When God wants a community reached, a family saved, a church alive, a business to bless people, he raises up a leader.

You?

God calls people to serve him.

The moment that you follow Jesus, truly follow Jesus, the moment you go 'all in', you start leading. A disciple who makes disciples, leads. The issues left are issues of geography (where?), demography (who?) and accountancy (how many?).

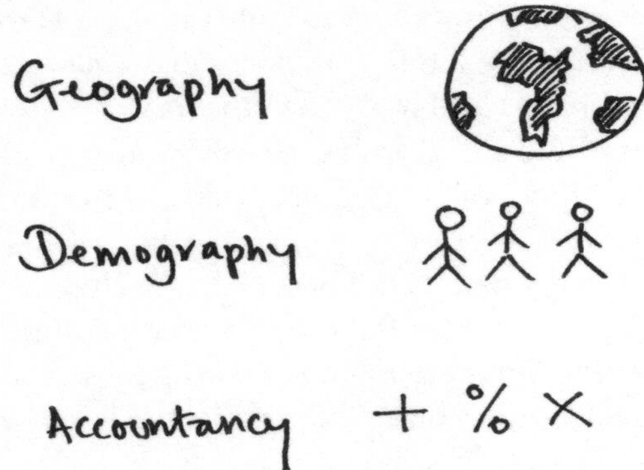

But you must lead. Or be suspicious that you're not really following.

TRACE A CIRCLE

You are The Project.

There is a story told of the evangelist Gypsy Smith. When asked about the secret to revival he responded with the advice to get on your knees, draw a chalk circle around yourself and only rise from your knees when the Lord has revived everything within that chalk circle.

The leadership project is *you*. The work God wants to do *through* you, he first wants to do *in* you.

Get on your knees. Recognise that your leadership will either lift or limit those that you are called to lead. So find some chalk. Get on your knees. Draw a circle. It's on you.

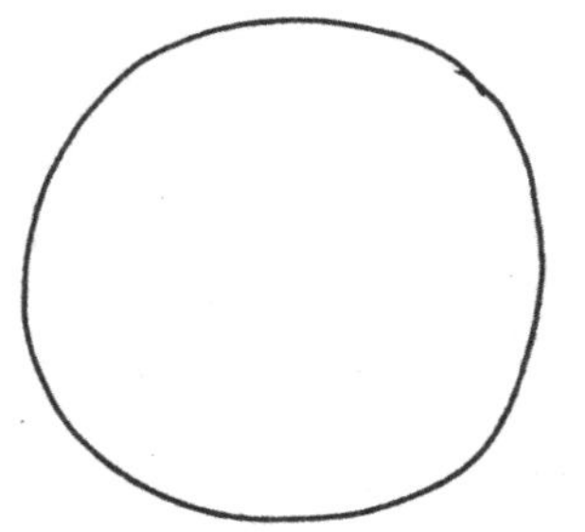

Trace a circle

Determine to grow.

Know yourself and grow yourself. What habits do you need to create? What changes do you need to make to your environment to be who God has called you to be?

The more you realise you are The Project, the better you will understand yourself, the better you will lead others. Whether you use Myers Briggs, the Enneagram, Belbin or a long walk and a talk with your friends – work out your wiring and your calling, and grow in understanding.

Understand your intellectual strengths and grow them. Read good things, listen to good things, go to good conferences. Choose well. Know the strengths and weaknesses of your emotional intelligence and stretch yourself relationally.

Determine to grow in your walk with Jesus. Your leadership is vital, but what is vital to your call to leadership is understanding that your primary call is to grow as a follower. Determine to get to know Jesus more, deeper, again and again and again.

Now ask the Lord to set you on fire, with a passion for him and a love for people.

Trace a circle. Recognise it's on you, no excuses.
Then get up.

DRAW A LINE

Look back.

Look back at your past, your journey thus far. Take off the rose-tinted sunglasses and look back. You will have regrets and scars and pain. Deal with your past. You don't need to carry that stuff into your future. That which you cannot confront, you will not conquer and you will undoubtedly carry. So, painful as it may be, look back. Dial back. Resolve to walk free. Who can help you with this? See a counsellor. Receive prayer. Ask forgiveness and give it. The past can so easily restrict and damage your future. Deal with it now. It will jump up and bite you later unless you deal with it now. So often the pain of the past destroys the potential of today and changes the paths of tomorrow. Damaged people tend to damage people. Healed leaders heal leaders. Look back and deal with the stuff that God is asking you to deal with. You can make a decision even as you read this, to refuse to bequeath to your children the things that you should cut out of your family line, your tribe, now.

Then move on.

With the past at your back, the future in your eyes and your focus on the now, move on. And *don't* look back. Draw a line, receive healing, accept forgiveness and stop glancing back. You will just get a stiff neck.

Draw a line. Let there be no regrets.

PLANT A STAKE

The secret to the success of your leadership will be the extent to which you identify the thing that God has got you for. What is your '*Yes!*'? You will never know what to do and what to say 'no' to until you identify your '*Yes!*' You have to know yourself to lead yourself.

Ask yourself: '*What has God got me for?*'

Not, 'What has the church got me for?', or 'What is everyone else doing?', or even 'What do people need?'

But '*What has God got me for?*'

How do you discover what God has got you for? How about you start by finding the triangulation point between your greatest complaint, your clearest dream and your biggest gift. Plant a stake.

Plant a stake

Plant a stake. That there may be no distractions.

Trace a circle.
Draw a line.
Plant a stake.

Now you are leading. But this is just the beginning of the journey. Your growing ability to help others lead – that's the heart of leadership. A legacy of circle tracers, line drawers and stake planters. You will look like Jesus and lead like Jesus and so will many others.

Read this book responsibly.

SET

You have to look at leadership through the eyes of the followers and you have to live the message. What I have learned is that people become motivated when you guide them to the source of their own power and when you make heroes out of employees who personify what you want to see in your organisation.

Anita Roddick, founder of Bodyshop

•

In the beginning was the Word, and the Word was with God, and the Word was God. He was with God in the beginning. Through him all things were made; without him nothing was made that has been made. In him was life, and that life was the light of all mankind. The light shines in the darkness, and the darkness has not overcome it.

John 1:1–5

The Word became flesh and made his dwelling among us. We have seen his glory, the glory of the one and only Son, who came from the Father, full of grace and truth.

John 1:14

In the beginning was the Word . . .

Through him all things were made . . .

He put on skin and moved into the neighborhood . . .

Full of grace and truth . . .

John 1

I would love to be Aragorn! In my fantasy world, Tolkien's brooding hero is me. I have less hair, my six pack is more hidden and I can't ride a horse. But it's *my* fantasy. I would love to be Aragorn, but I've got to be Gandalf.

In *The Hero with a Thousand Faces*,[1] Joseph Campbell suggests that all the stories of our world – all films, sagas and epic tales, from *The Lord of the Rings* to *Harry Potter* – are based on a single 'monomyth'. This monomyth is the hero's journey: the story of a hero and a quest, a threshold crossed, a test and a sacrifice, a mentor and a bounty won and a blessing for everyone.

It is of course in leadership that we get to be the hero of our own stories and win the bounty for the sake of many. But Jesus' model of leadership is a little different: here we get to be the mentor serving and apprenticing a whole generation of heroes. We get to be Gandalf, apprenticing a generation of Aragorns into new hero journeys.

LEADERSHIP IN CRISIS

In just about every arena of western life and culture, leadership is in question. Books and blogs, articles and opinions about leadership abound. And yet our political leaders govern with record low popularity ratings, our football managers have shorter shelf lives than ever and our business leaders are pilloried for their exaggerated bonus culture.

At the same time, the rising generation of Jesus followers appears increasingly suspicious and disillusioned with political leaders, frustrated and at odds with family leadership, and unsure of the need or value of spiritual leadership.

Yet we crave it.

Tall poppy

There is a widely recognised syndrome, particularly prevalent in UK culture, known as 'Tall Poppy Syndrome' – where any

---

[1] Joseph Campbell, *The Hero with a Thousand Faces* (Bollingen Foundation, 1949).

'poppy' that rises above its peers, any leader that has earned stature in some way, is quickly cut down. No poppy should rise above the other poppies.

Why is this the case? Why is this true, even for the people of God?

Can it be a collective bad experience of leadership? A collective bad memory of bad leadership that has caused an anti-leadership reaction? Maybe, but perhaps the problem runs deeper. Without wishing to suggest a weird conspiracy I find myself wondering if somewhere, sown deep in our cultural philosophy, is a subtle undermining of a gift of God.

The shadow of feudalism

For about a thousand years, the enduring political structure in Europe was feudalism. A feudal lord owned everything in a region: property, land and peasants. He held all power and made all decisions. Roles were set: peasants served the lord by working his land and paying him taxes. Lords were supposed to be benefactors, looking after their people. By the end of the first world war, through a combination of famine, conflict and the industrialisation of a continent, there had been a redefining of status and relationship, and the shackles of feudalism had been almost completely thrown off.

It is fascinating that the rejection of European feudalism by the United States, embodied in the Declaration of Independence, resulted in an implicit philosophy that 'everyone can be a Lord'. But Europeans, in contrast, assumed that 'everyone can be a peasant'.

If we think like feudal lords, we can act with a sense of entitlement and patronage, but where a whole culture has been raised to believe that they are peasants, encouraged 'not to get ahead of themselves' and discouraged to believe for more or better, people become suffocated by 'poverty thinking'. In this environment, leadership is viewed with suspicion, and embraced with fear. Only the feudal lords feel equipped to lead, and often they do it badly.

The vestiges of liberalism

One important development of the Enlightenment was the growing philosophy of individualism. A new belief in the dignity and autonomy of the individual soon led to the idea that I should be totally free and totally responsible for me and my decisions. Taking this to extremes has undermined the power of community and done subtle damage to the concept of Jesus-leadership.

Just recently I sat drinking coffee with an emerging leader, one who is clearly gifted and called. When I challenged him about his leadership calling he expressed that view that for him the bottom line was that he was only responsible for his walk with Jesus, nobody else's. At the end of the day the only account he would have to give was for his own stuff. He is a product of a culture of extreme individualism and hesitancy around leadership. And yet the truth is, he has been given much *and* much will be expected of him (Luke 12:48). He teaches much and will be judged accordingly (James 3:1). He and I and you will account for what we have done with what we are given (2 Corinthians 5:10). It's never just you and Jesus and Jesus and you. It starts there, but never ends there. You are not free to decide to do whatever you think is right without reference to anyone else. Your relationship with God is personal but not private.

The echoes of socialism

The priesthood of all believers is a beautiful foundational doctrine of ministry and leadership explaining that there are now no earthly mediators between God and man (Matthew 27:51), that we can approach God directly, through our Lord Jesus Christ (1 Timothy 2:5) the one great high priest whose sacrifice was once and for all (Hebrews 4:14–16, 10:12), and that all believers are chosen to offer up spiritual sacrifices (1 Peter 2:5, 9). If applied perfectly, the priesthood of all believers would see the 'full mobilisation of the entire body of Christ for the total work of God', and the world would be transformed by the gospel.

However, when you misunderstand this teaching to mean 'anyone can do anything', your praxis tends to be more informed by Marxism than Jesus. The radical freedom and cultural reformation of the 1960s has compounded our leadership issues.

The moment you start to really follow Christ, you lead: you stand in the gap, you minister, you disciple. This is a fundamental tenet of discipleship. Practised wrongly it just becomes a pseudo hippy commune – anyone can do whatever they want. The truth is that we are all equal in value – but unequal in calling and unique in gifting.

My early taste of Christianity was in a 'pass the leadership around' culture, pass the Bible study leadership, whose turn is it to lead worship? The subtle results of this philosophy are:

Nobody should lead anybody.
Who are you to lead anybody?
Anyone can lead anything.

ZIG ZAG

Whether your experience was damaging, disabling, frustrating, limiting or neutral, more often than not we evidence a dysfunctional view of leadership. So each generation attempts a corrective. But it attempts to change up against the wrong thing.

A reactive overcorrection.

We change up against last year's abuse. Last year's mistake. Last year's inadequacy.

We zig zag.

We run from command-control leadership structures, where hierarchy and submission rules, and respond with collaborative flat structures, where change is hard to come by and inertia reigns.

We zig zag.

We do it with theology. One generation's conservative evangelicalism becomes the next generation's charismatic. We do it with style and praxis. From structured formality to organic informality. And we do it with leadership.

And the problem is we are changing up against the wrong thing. We change up against the wrong template.

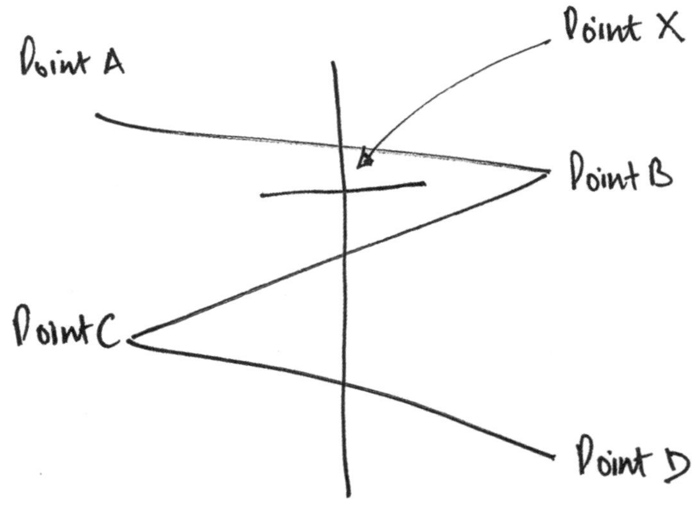

THE MODEL IS JESUS

What if the model of all great leadership is Jesus? What if he really is the template? What would it look like to change up against him?

His words, his works, his way. Let's call this 'Jesus-leadership'.

Now please don't hear what I'm not saying – I'm not suggesting we ditch the wisdom of the likes of Aristotle and Gandhi and

Churchill and Mandela and Gladwell and Collins or any of the leadership gurus currently available for hire. No, it is rather more that, where there is anything helpful about these guys and their teaching, its root and source and inspiration is in fact … Jesus. See, Jesus is not just perfect humanity and perfect theology. Jesus is perfect leadership.

To lead well, in whatever circumstances we are called to lead, we have to go back to the source.

From the very start of his ministry the leadership philosophy of Jesus is set.

For him.
For me.
For you.

> *In the beginning was the Word, and the Word was with God, and the Word was God.*
>
> John 1:1

Jesus-leadership is a statement

In the Greek the word is *logos*. And what John is doing, in a really quite brilliant way, is combining two ancient thought systems around one word. For the ancient Greeks *logos* was the principle shaping and ordering and directing the universe, and for the ancient Hebrews it was the breath of God, active in the forming of the world from nothing into something, from abstract nothing into substantive something. For us, what is a word, anyway? A word is an audible or visual expression of a thought or idea, an idea that is incommunicable until put into a word.

Leadership is a word, a statement. It is a statement of intent, a statement of purpose.

Jesus-leadership is a statement that is purposeful

When I arrived in Edinburgh one of the earliest conversations I had went something like this:

> *'The most important consideration of your ministry, young man,' (in those days I could have been mistaken for one), 'is that there is a church called Morningside Baptist Church when you are dead and gone that still exists and meets at Holy Corner.'*
>
> *'With all due respect, sir,' I replied, 'I could not disagree with you more. The most important thing about my ministry is that lives have been changed, the city is transformed, and that God is being glorified. What we call ourselves and where we meet are secondary and transitory issues.'*

So often the leadership roles that we are asked to take up are roles of preservation, not of speculation. There has to be something more than preserving what has been or it cannot call itself leadership.

> There has to be growth.
> There has to be multiplication.
> There have to be dreams being fulfilled.
> There have to be purposes worked out.
> There has to be transformation in our culture.

... or is it even leadership?

What is changing?

Jesus-leadership is a statement that creates

> *Through him all things were made; without him nothing was made that has been made.*
>
> John 1:3

Leadership is a statement that is purposeful, that brings order – that creates. This is leadership beyond management; this leadership reaches for something more than what already exists. This leadership is catalytic. It expects situations to be better, teams to be different, something to be birthed, because it is the leadership of Jesus. Put a leader in the room and there is purpose, creativity, change, multiplication.

This leadership is an art form. It creates something where there was nothing.

What is getting added, changed, created, birthed? What is going to exist that did not exist because you walk in this kind of leadership? This leadership is not understated, or hidden. Not embarrassed, or shy, or hesitating.

What is there now, that wasn't there before, because you are involved?

Jesus-leadership is a statement wrapped in humanity

Leadership is an embodied statement. It is incarnational. God sent Jesus on mission. You could say God needed a body back then and he needs one now.

The Word became flesh and made his dwelling among us.

John 1:14

He put on skin and moved into the neighbourhood.

John 1:14 (The Message)

Leadership is a statement wrapped in humanity. He put on flesh and moved into the neighbourhood. Leadership is a statement wrapped in humility. The flesh that he put on was unlikely flesh, it was baby flesh, it was peasant flesh, it was Middle Eastern oppressed flesh and the 'hood he moved into was at best lower middle class non-influential – by any measure.

Leadership is an embodied statement. It is involved. Leadership for Jesus is hands on, down and dirty. It is not removed and consulting, it is practical and modelling.

He put on flesh.
Flesh and blood God.
Immanuel God.
God-with-us leadership.

Jesus walked the dust paths of Judea as rabbi, and his followers were disciples, *talmidim.* He was following an ancient tradition: around the age of fifteen, a truly outstanding student might apply to a local rabbi to become his disciple – if selected, if the rabbi felt the student had the potential to become *like* him, he would be introduced into the rabbi's household to live and learn his yoke, his teaching, to imitate him. Disciples would learn through imitation over many years as they walked in his dust. They would learn his words, they would do his works and they would walk in his way – it was an intense, personal relationship. The most zealous disciples would follow so closely behind the rabbi that they would be said to be covered in the dust that kicked up as he walked. Finally, at the age of perhaps thirty, they might be ready to become rabbis themselves.

Jesus' model of leadership is apprenticeship. Not just obedience to his teaching – and Jesus did a lot of teaching – but practising his activity and imitating his style. This was how higher education happened – it was all to do with proximity to the rabbi and openness to his yoke. It was apprenticeship in the life of Jesus. We may find this quite difficult to comprehend because our culture has all but lost the tradition of apprenticeship and neglected the central role of imitation in learning. We have adopted a style of education focused on information to be learned and absorbed and innovated upon.

Jesus-leadership is apprenticeship in his life. It is apprenticing other people into the life that we have inherited. It is relational, necessarily so: it requires proximity, it takes time and it is all about people.

Jesus is highly intentional in his selection of his succession team. In fact, it is almost the first thing that he does when he starts to proclaim the kingdom of God (John 1:35–50). He calls men to himself.[2] He calls them to himself and then spends three years apprenticing them in his life with the clear

[2] Let's not get distracted by the fact that they are all men. Many of the significant leaders of Jesus' entourage were rich women and a number of the vital leaders of the early church were not male.

intention that he is going to hand the whole of his ministry on to them.

Jesus-leadership is the way of restoration

Amid the religious leadership of the day, Jesus' leadership stood out. The Jewish religious leaders either blended in or separated off. The Pharisees and Essenes were separatists. Pharisees lived in society but tried at all times to distance themselves from culture – their name meant 'separatist'. The Essenes removed themselves completely, they were 'isolationist'. The Sadducees and Herodians were 'blenders'. Faith for them was more of a private matter.[3]

Jesus' third way was the way of restoration, thoughtfully and wholeheartedly engaging with his world. He loved it and confronted it and lived for its transformation. Jesus-leadership is ordering and shaping.

Where does my leadership make a difference to the world? In what way does it restore and free people?

Jesus-leadership is a liberating statement

'... *full of grace and truth.*'

John 1:14

Jesus knew that those he led would not only live but grow and learn to lead in a high support – high challenge culture. Grace and truth. He was full of it.

Jesus begins his public leadership with the words 'Come, follow me' (Matthew 4:19) and brings his earthly leadership journey to a close with the challenge to 'Go into all the world' (Mark 16:15). Throughout the whole of his time with his disciples he is calibrating support and challenge, come and go, grace and truth.

---

[3] This is described well in Gabe Lyons, *The Next Christians, Seven Ways You Can Live the Gospel and Restore the World,* (Multnomah UK, 2012).

Grace – Truth.
Both – And.

Jesus-leadership holds these together, constantly. It liberates leaders, liberates followers. It frees people to become all they are called to be, to run with the dreams that God has placed in their hearts.

If we don't hold both together in equal tension, we end up dominating or protecting, rather than liberating. Dominating because we speak truth without grace and over-challenge. Protecting because we give grace without truth and over-support. Liberation and restoration happen in a grace–truth dynamic.[4]

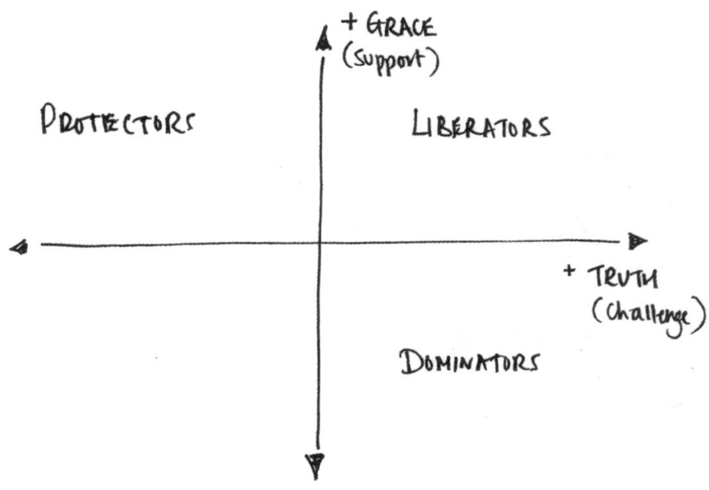

Your leadership needs to be a statement of purpose that changes situations. Your leadership must be active and involved.

[4] Mike Breen and the 3DM team, *Building a Discipling Culture: How to release a missional movement by discipling people like Jesus did* (3DM, 2011), p 18.

Bringing freedom and restoration. This is the leadership of Jesus.

Read on.

There is a leadership tool which takes elements of Jesus' leadership and puts them together into progressive steps – I have found it useful, as have many business leaders. We call it 'The Discipleship Square' and it looks like this:

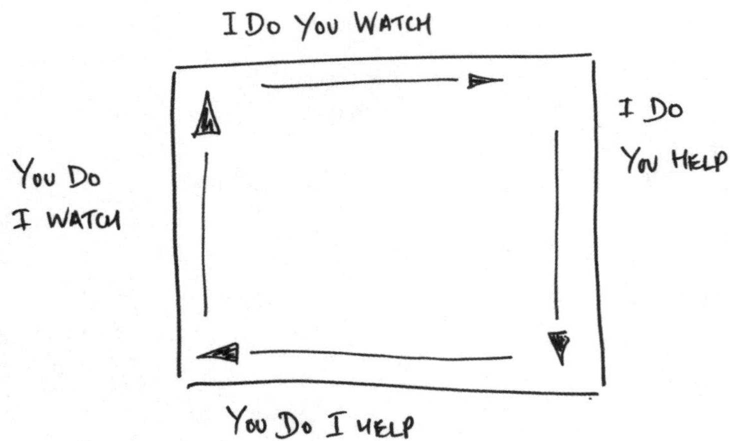

1. *I do – you watch.* Allow your leaders to watch you. Jesus' disciples would have spent hours, days, months simply watching Jesus in every situation. From when his call to 'Come and you will see' (John 1:39) to the Wedding at Cana (John 2:2) to cleansing the temple (John 2:17) they watched and learned.

2. *I do – you help.* It's useful to ask an apprentice to do parts of a task before giving them responsibility for the whole thing. In the feeding of the five thousand Jesus asked his disciples to hand out the bread and fish (Matthew 14:19).
3. *You do – I help.* Let them have a go. Probably a small thing first. Jesus said 'Whoever can be trusted with very little can also be trusted with much …' (Luke 16:10). Be ready to step in if you need to. Jesus stepped in when his disciples couldn't cast out the demon from the little boy. But he also explained to them afterwards what had gone wrong (Mark 9:14–29; Matthew 17).
4. *You do – I watch.* Let go, stand back and watch. This is possibly the hardest part. Jesus did it. The only thing you have to do is to be ready to encourage and cheer on – and take the blame if something goes wrong.

Discipleship – apprenticeship in the life of Jesus – is the only way to learn Jesus-leadership.

Having loved his own who were in the world, he loved them to the end...

He poured water into a basin and began to wash his disciples' feet ...

John 13

1.

SERVE

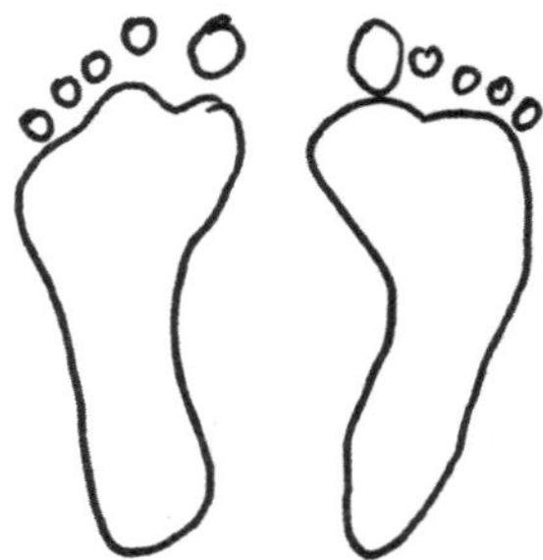

Everybody can be great, because everybody can serve. You don't have to have a college degree to serve. You don't have to make your subject and your verb agree to serve. You don't have to know about Plato and Aristotle to serve … You only need a heart full of grace, a soul generated by love. And you can be that servant.

Martin Luther King

•

When he had finished washing their feet, he put on his clothes and returned to his place. 'Do you understand what I have done for you?' he asked them. 'You call me "Teacher" and "Lord", and rightly so, for that is what I am. Now that I, your Lord and Teacher, have washed your feet, you also should wash one another's feet. I have set you an example that you should do as

I have done for you. Very truly I tell you, no servant is greater than his master, nor is a messenger greater than the one who sent him. Now that you know these things, you will be blessed if you do them.'

John 13:12–17

My father was a Baptist pastor; he went to Spurgeon's College. My brother is a Baptist pastor; he went to Spurgeon's College. My uncle is a Baptist pastor, and he went to Spurgeon's. My brother-in-law was a Baptist pastor, and he went to Spurgeon's. You could cut me …

So at the age of twenty-six, after leaving Spurgeon's College, I went to be the assistant pastor in a Baptist church in Leeds. It was brilliant. I got to be involved in a church plant, and it grew. I got to be involved in a church resurrection, and it grew. I got to be involved in a church congregation amongst students and it grew massively, and we had to do two services on a Sunday evening.

And then the senior pastor, who was amazing, left. And I became the pastor. Which was perfect. I was in my early thirties and I was so ready for this.

But I so *wasn't* ready for it.

It all seemed like it was going to go great. And then things were said and things were done that probably shouldn't have been said and shouldn't have been done. Maybe you know how that goes. There were a number of things that needed to change in order for the church to grow in terms of mission – and I almost certainly wasn't mature enough to handle it. I hadn't had enough leadership experience. Those who opposed me were all wrong and I was all right, and … I resigned. I mean, it probably took about three months, but eventually, I resigned.

We lived in a manse.
And we had four young kids.
I had no job now and no home.
As my wife pointed out.
After I'd resigned.

The issue was me.
I would have argued, robustly, that the issue was *not* me.
But it was, at least significantly, me.

It usually is.
As a leader, you are The Project.

God needed to do a pretty large number in my life, and I was going to have to allow him, if I was to be the Jesus-leader he wanted. I had a love for the crowds, which led me to live for the approval of others, and an ambition that was often more about me than him. I had a fear of being out of control, which caused me to shut down the activity of the Holy Spirit, rendering myself, and many of those I led, powerless. I had a predisposition for unhealthy competition, which made me jealous of other people's ministries, and, to compound it all, I had a minor messiah complex, which needed me to be at the centre of my world.

I was theoretically qualified to lead this church.
And wholly unqualified to do it like Jesus.

God met me in many ways. In worship meetings, through wise people, in challenges, through his word. God had a big task ahead of him to free me to lead in a way that would free others to lead.

There is a deep work that has to happen for Jesus-leadership to emerge, a deep work of the heart. I am The Project, and so are you. There is something that is supposed to happen *in* you – if anything is going to shine *through* you. The transformation God wants to do through you, he first has to do *in* you.

You are The Project; you are the model: because this is the leadership of Jesus.

You are The Project; The Project is you: you, learning to love, and you, learning to serve.

leader... you are the Project

So, John Chapter 13.

Jesus is now in the upper room with his disciples. This is holy ground. If all Scripture is God-breathed, this is like God's deep breath. Jesus is in the last few days before the cross and this is his opportunity to intentionally pass on to them the stuff of leadership that they are going to have to carry when he leaves. This is Jesus reminding his team of the things they have seen and experienced and underlining the things they might forget.

Listen in…

> *It was just before the Passover Festival. Jesus knew that the hour had come for him to leave this world and go to the Father. Having loved his own who were in the world, he loved them to the end.*
>
> *The evening meal was in progress, and the devil had already prompted Judas, the son of Simon Iscariot, to betray Jesus. Jesus knew that the Father had put all things under his power, and that he had come from God and was returning to God; so he got up from the meal, took off his outer clothing, and wrapped a towel round his waist. After that, he poured water into a basin and began to wash his disciples' feet, drying them with the towel that was wrapped round him.*
>
> John 13:1–5

John tells us this is a highly significant moment – Jesus wants to show his disciples 'the full extent of his love' (NIV 1984), or 'the end goal of his love'. John combines two Greek words, *eis* (moving into) and *telos*, (purpose, consummation, end goal) which get translated 'moving towards the end'.

This is it, people! The aim and ambition of Jesus' love for his disciples, for us.

So what does he do?

What would you do?

I would do something spectacular. I would do a raising from the dead, a creative miracle, a miraculous healing. But Jesus does something almost … disappointing. He takes off his outer clothing and washes his disciples' feet.

Your feet are probably horrible. I have no doubt that mine are. But they are probably clean. Feet, back in the day, were almost certainly filthy – in the summer the streets were like dust bowls. In the winter they were like quagmires. And all the time they were the sewers. Feet cleaning duty was vital but disgusting, the task of the lowest of the low in the house – almost never a Jewish servant.

And these disciples were not even particularly worthy of such a show of humility. Jesus knew all that would happen – he knew the running away, the abandonment, the denial, the betrayal. He *knew* his disciples. He knew Peter. He knew Judas.

These disciples.
He knows them.
And he washes their feet.

Jesus is staging an incredible learning laboratory for his prototype disciples: *they* are The Project. In about three hundred years this project is going to be so successful that fifty percent of the known world will also classify themselves as disciples. But at the moment it is just these disciples. And *they* are The Project.

Jesus is not, at this moment, building a church.[5] He is making disciples. These disciples are to be disciples who make disciples. Church will be the result. But discipleship is the cause and the way. Jesus' goal for your leadership is that you should be a disciple who makes disciples.

Jesus wants to make a definitive statement about his leadership, his lordship, his love, the full extent of his love. So what does he do? He doesn't stand on a platform and open a Powerpoint presentation. He stoops low with a towel and a bowl.

---

[5] And remember that Jesus never asked us as leaders to build the church or even to preserve it. He appears to reserve this privilege for himself – remember his commission of Peter at Caesarea Philippi? '*I* will build my Church.' (Matthew 16:18).

What he wants to communicate to his followers is that he loves them. It is grace and love that define his leadership, not power and position. The heart of his ministry is love. The way he feels about people is love.

Love leads.

This is a freeing and liberating thought for disciples that were used to a world dominated and divided by the command and control leadership of the Roman occupiers and the power manipulation leadership of the Jewish religious leaders.

Jesus offers another way, a new kind of leadership.

The towel and the bowl has never been more relevant as a leadership model. In a world where even spiritual leadership is shot through with positioning and power games; in a church which is not immune to career manoeuvres and control plays; where leaders are burnt out and beaten up enough to just give in, and where members are restricted or treated as consumers. He offers another way.

Jesus leads with love. He's looking for leadership that will love and serve a broken world. This is leadership. Love and serve.

There are only too many church leaders who are lonely and broken and have lost the passion they once had for what God has called them to do. Perhaps you know one. Perhaps you *are* one. There are only too many churches that feel beaten up and misunderstood by the leadership called to oversee them, too many people that feel used and too many leaders that feel frustrated.

The problem lies in a misunderstanding of leadership. To lead is to serve because leadership is love.

And right here is my problem. I'm not sure I can love like this. Or serve like him. People are irritating and smelly and unappreciative and feel entitled and are generally difficult to lead.

And so am I.

love starts with loved

In order to give Jesus' love, the disciples need to receive Jesus' love. Serve starts with love, and love starts with loved.

Jesus approaches Simon Peter to wash his feet. And Peter is offended. I might be. Surely this should be the other way around – I should wash Jesus' feet. Jesus says to Peter 'You do not realise now what I am doing, but later you will understand.' In true Peter style, he declares, 'You shall never wash my feet.' Jesus counters with one of those very, very scary verses of Scripture, 'Unless I wash you, you have no part with me' (John 13:7, 8).

You can't give what you haven't received.

You can't flow with what you don't know.

I imagine there to be a deafening silence in the room when this is spoken. And there is one in my heart when I write this. This is colossal.

Love starts with loved.

In my experience of leadership there are two kinds of people who are really hard to help. Those who are always on the take – they want something for free, they watch the clock, they are always after a pay rise. And those who are always on the give, who will never receive, who cannot be blessed.

Both are actually forms of pride. Both find it difficult to receive love. Both postures militate against the stoop, the towel and the bowl. Leadership, true Jesus-leadership – stoop, towel and bowl leadership – begins with humility. And humility starts with dependence. I need love to give love.

You have to allow him to wash you.

Once,
a thousand times,
every day.

Continually. Let him heal you. Let him love you. Let him forgive you. Let him wash you.

And Peter, who is an all-or-nothing kind of guy, says give me a bath then. I'm all in, jacuzzi me up. But Jesus says, you are clean, let me wash your feet.

> *'Then, Lord,' Simon Peter replied, 'not just my feet but my hands and my head as well!'*
>
> *Jesus answered, 'Those who have had a bath need only to wash their feet; their whole body is clean.'*
>
> John 13:9, 10

As you walk through this life, apprenticed by Jesus – as you follow hard after him – your feet are going to get dirty. You are going to mess up and slip up sometimes, and you're going to get hurt. You're going to need forgiveness if you are going to give forgiveness, healing if you are going to offer healing, and fresh starts if you are going to offer clean slates. It's not the same as going right back to the beginning – you won't need a full bath or a full baptism again – just a foot wash, or the love goes sour and the grace fades.

The love that you have to offer must be Jesus' love or it's not going to work. Those I lead – they don't want *my* love, because my love is impatient and not very kind. My love is limited and self-absorbed, my love is transactional, sometimes. But his love is perfect. Unconditional, patient and kind.

My job as a leader is to be a dealer in his love, a vessel of his love. So I need to be filled, again and again, that I might flow. I'm a conduit not a bucket. Leaders flow with love. Channel love. Be hungry for more.

Find the places where you can just sit under a power shower of his affection. It might be a particular place, a familiar conference, a trusted mentor or a book that brings life. I don't really care about the details, I just care for you and those you lead, they need fresh love, channelled love, not yesterday's love. Do what you have to do.

Find music that plugs you into the love of God for you. Sit at the feet of those who speak grace from the book of grace, those who remind you of grace. And receive love. I have long given up being too embarrassed to run to the prayer ministry team in my (or any other) church for prayer. I am desperate to stay connected to the flow of love that pours from the heart of the foot-washer to me, one who is called to wash feet.

Love starts with loved.

OWN NOTHING

As I write the world's largest taxi service, *Uber,* owns no cars. The world's biggest Bed and Breakfast provider, *AirBnB*, owns no houses, and the world's largest movie house, *Netflix,* owns no cinemas. The growing disruption of the digital revolution is fundamentally undermining the concept of ownership. Ownership has been overrated. It feels very disturbing, and yet, in a sense all we are discovering is the practice of a far more ancient biblical principle called 'stewardship'. Jesus-leaders carry it tangibly.

One of the biggest problems of any leadership is control. And at the root of much control is the false idea that as a leader it is *your* ministry, it is *your* church, it is *your* calling, it is *your* vision.

One of the first commands that God ever gave anyone was to steward everything. To care for the garden, to tend it and cultivate it. Not to own it, buy it, get a mortgage on it or develop it for financial gain. Jesus refers frequently to the leadership of the housekeeper, *oikonomos*, and both Peter and Paul use this same metaphor for church leadership and the administration of spiritual gifts.[6] My role as leader is to steward that which God has given, and still owns, for this generation and the next. I hold it in trust. I hold it in keeping for him and for others. I hold it lightly.

---

[6] Luke 12:42, 16:1–3; 1 Corinthians 4:1–2; 1 Peter 4:10.

It is not my pulpit – which means others can have a go in it.

It is not my boardroom – which means others can have opinions in it.

It is not my vision – so others can contribute to it.

It is not mine, it's his.

And one day I will pass it on completely. But now I must pass it on in pieces.

My call as a leader is not to get those who follow to serve my passion and my dream. Rather it is to provoke and release and equip the dreams that God has already placed in the hearts of the people he has called me to lead. It is to serve *them*. Can you imagine the potential released in the people of God if everyone learned to run with these dreams, because those called to lead had learned to effectively provoke and creatively facilitate the call of God for everyone?

In recent years there seem to have been two equal and opposite approaches to ministry leadership training. A previous generation of Christian leaders were trained in a command and control style of leadership. Of course we would never have called it this, but this is what it was. It was designed to create a hierarchical environment where the leader was in control. Effectively he became a little pope, a benevolent dictator. He was chairman of any important committee and found a way to get his way (it was usually a he!).

In contrast I was trained in an era where the reaction to that suffocating approach was an implicit abdication of leadership. Flat structures which generated limited vision and achieved equally limited breakthrough.

There must be a better way.

There is.

Jesus' way.

THE TRAINING GROUND OVER THE STADIUM

It's more about the training ground and the eleven, than the stadium and the 60,000.

So often, leaders who are regarded as significant are those who are magnetic, who attract, often by their personality. It's true, but dangerous. The foundational ambition of the Jesus-leader is the developing of the leadership of others. It has more in common with the coach than the star performer. It works itself out on the training ground and in the dressing room, often far away from the floodlights of acclaim, so that others can thrive, can star and can shine.

In the church I lead we have become increasingly determined as leaders to identify, provoke, equip and release the leadership potential in others. Often to the apparent detriment of superficial reputation but, we think, to the benefit of the kingdom of God. It is not primarily important how many children come to the children's club but it is fundamentally important that our parents are being encouraged and trained and resourced to be the best parents they can be and that our children are growing up in extended families. It is not of first importance how many people are showing up to worship on Sunday but it is of primary concern how many of those who called our church home are tooled up to hear and obey the voice of God and to pursue the vision he has placed in them.

TRAIN YOUR MUSCLES

If you want to become physically strong you need to train. Training entails repetitions, pain and sweat, so that muscles might become effective, quick and strong. Growing leadership happens the same way. You must train your servant muscles.

One of the great modern inspirations of servant leadership was Chuck Smith, the founder of the Calvary Chapel movement. Right up until soon before his death in his eighties he could be found walking around the campus of his church, picking up litter, serving. He would apprentice leaders who came asking to be trained for church planting by first making them sweep leaves and clean bathrooms. He was helping them develop the muscles of leadership.

Leader, if you have not done your time lifting chairs, locking up or cleaning buildings and floors, you probably have not grown enough muscle to enable you to do any heavy servant lifting. And if you are now beyond cleaning a toilet or washing a floor you are probably beyond Jesus-leadership. Sort it. If you have the privilege and insight to run a leadership development or internship programme, then absolutely ensure that at the heart it contains a course of simple service, or you will be creating leaders who are in danger of missing the very heart of God.

Set your heart

What is the collective noun for a gathering of church leaders?

(a) A moan?
(b) A sigh?
(c) A resignation?

Have you noticed how at ministers' gatherings we quickly start to moan about our lot: the pay, the leadership group, the stubborn congregation, and everyone sympathises. Sadly, we just end up demoralising one another!

When my father was alive I would often use him as a sounding board for my criticisms of everyone else, who was wrong and why, and the church that was killing me. On one occasion he said to me 'Karl, have they crucified you yet?' Needless to say the tone of future conversations changed dramatically.

Servants ultimately will die for those they serve.
So set your heart for service.
Set your heart to die.

Fix your filter

The culture that you demonstrate is the culture that you cultivate; the culture that you cultivate is the culture you will propagate. It goes from you, to your disciples, to their disciples. And this is vital, because those you lead will only get it and do it once they've seen it. We need to shift from functional-style leadership, where leaders are CEOs of their organisations, to family leadership where life and style and culture are caught not just taught; where leaders are mothers and fathers looking to grow up, equip and release children to be better than them.

I have four daughters who I love dearly, and I do all in my power to provide an environment of training, equipping and encouragement for the development of all the potential that God has placed in them. I have many, many more 'adopted' sons and daughters, members of my team, who I love dearly and have the same ambitions for. It's not so different … is it?

Who makes the noise?

Benjamin Zander is Conductor and Music Director of the Boston Philharmonic Youth Orchestra, and an expert in Mahler and Beethhoven. In one of the most watched TED talks ever,[7] he speaks of an epiphany, midway through his career, when he 'got' this kind of leadership. He realised that his was the name on the front of the cd, his was the photo, baton raised, and yet he never made a noise. His job, like every great leader, is to enable others to make the right noise – to leverage their ability to make a beautiful sound. He speaks memorably of the time he realised that when his orchestra performed well, when they performed with grace and feeling and really connected with the music and the people, the eyes of the audience would shine. His ambition is to conduct his orchestra so well that they make the eyes of the audience shine.

Leader, we get the joy of enabling others to make a beautiful sound. We get to serve, they get to play, and the world's eyes shine.

Jesus takes a step back from what he is doing to teach his slightly bewildered disciples, and asks them: Do you understand what I just did? What I am doing is being the model, setting you an

---

[7] http://www.ted.com/talks/benjamin_zander_on_music_and_passion

example. You should do as I have done. Serve people, touch people, demonstrate the kingdom, love the unlovely, take the lowest place. Be me. And you will be blessed if you do.

What we are being told by the greatest leader who ever lived is that he wants us to look like him. He wants us to act like him. We are to go and become a revelation of him everywhere we go. And that is going to look like love.

You are The Project. You are The Project and then you become The Model. And then everyone else is The Project.

Who are your heroes?

How have you let Jesus wash your feet recently?

How intentional are you in your serving? How can you wash the feet of the team you serve?

Who has enough proximity to your life to imitate you?

Do you have a life worth imitating?

'My Father's house has many rooms'...

'I am the way and the truth and the life. No one comes to the Father except through me'...

'Whoever believes in me will do the works I have been doing, and they will do even greater things than these...'

John 14

2.

SECURE

'Do not let your hearts be troubled. You believe in God; believe also in me. My Father's house has many rooms; if that were not so, would I have told you that I am going there to prepare a place for you? And if I go and prepare a place for you, I will come back and take you to be with me that you also may be where I am. You know the way to the place where I am going.'

Thomas said to him, 'Lord, we don't know where you are going, so how can we know the way?'

Jesus answered, 'I am the way and the truth and the life. No one comes to the Father except through me.'

John 14:1–6

•

'Very truly I tell you, whoever believes in me will do the works I have been doing, and they will do even greater things than these, because I am going to the Father. And I will do whatever you ask in my name, so that the Father may be glorified in the Son. You may ask me for anything in my name, and I will do it.'

John 14:12–14

As I write this, I am conscious of a significant sense of anxiety. I'm leading a church with hundreds of people looking to me for inspiration and security. I'm leading dozens of people who are expecting me to be strong and to know the way. I'm attempting to pioneer a movement of discipleship, offering hope to churches and individuals who are looking for support that I feel ill-equipped to offer. At the same time, for whatever reason, I have a number of opportunities to speak in a variety of different places. All of those invitations are expecting a 'yes'. And the ones I respond positively to are assuming I will 'knock the ball out of the park'. I have a wife I love and four adult daughters who all need me to be Dad. A family who need me to provide for them, physically, spiritually, emotionally and financially (I am gnawingly aware of a potential wedding bill). I'm pretty sure I have a wasps' nest in my attic … and then there is this book that I am trying to write on leadership.

It may well be that I am doing too much. And we will talk about focus later. But feeling troubled, and leaning towards anxiety and fear is a constant and significant temptation. And here is the thing. I have *every reason* to lean towards anxiety.

As a leader, there will be many times when you have *every reason* to lean towards anxiety. You may occasionally think there has never been stress like you are experiencing right now, there has never been pressure like that which you are under at this moment, there has never been opposition like you are facing. And then, every news bulletin, every twitter feed, every parenting heartache, every pastoral conundrum, every strategic decision has a stress value attached to it, and someone in your care is probably looking to you for help to deal with their mounting stress. You either have to grit your teeth and deal with it, or run away crying.

Leader, anxiety is going to be a strong temptation.
Jesus says, do not be anxious.

So, John 14.

> *'Do not let your hearts be troubled. You believe in God; believe also in me. My Father's house has many rooms; if that were not so, would I have told you that I am going there to prepare a place for you? And if I go and prepare a place for you, I will come back and take you to be with me that you also may be where I am. You know the way to the place where I am going.'*
>
> John 14:1–4

BELIEVE

Remember, back in John 13, we learned that Jesus knew who he was, that he was from the Father and he was returning to the Father. Jesus knew he was a son. Jesus knew he was a son and this gave him the security he needed to humble himself, to wash feet, to care for others, even knowing all that lay ahead for him.

Now Jesus starts to teach his disciples. He has told them he is about to go away, and the disciples are about to experience the most disturbing and violent events of their lives. The temptation to feel not only troubled, but abandoned, let down and orphaned, must have been overwhelming. They had *every reason* to lean towards anxiety.

So Jesus provides an antidote for anxiety in leadership and life. He says trust me: 'believe also in me'. Not just 'believe what I said' but

> *in* me,
> in who I am,
> in who I say I am,
> in who you have come to know me to be.

He says, 'You believe in God, believe also in me.' Put the whole weight of your life on me. I won't abandon you.

The antidote to anxiety is to *believe*. To believe his teaching, yes, but more than that, to believe *in him*. The Son. To believe in who he is, what you know him to be like, who you have come to know him to be. Believe in him, and trust him. It's a choice. It's a decision. It's an act of faith.

Know the Father

Enter with me into this passage – can you hear the whisper of Jesus? Don't be anxious, don't be troubled, it's going to be ok, there is another way.

See, there is a Father.

Jesus is reminding the disciples of something that could easily be forgotten. He is reminding them that this God – the one that you have known as being the power source in the universe, the one that you have known to be the Lord of the Angel Armies, the one that you have to revere, the one that you have to worship – he's *your Father.*

And he cares.

Even about details.

You don't have to be troubled or anxious or upset because he's got your back, he really has. He really knows your situation – he knows about the book deadline and the speaking invitations, he made the wasps in the attic, he understands the neighbour's cancer, he knows the heartache, and he knows the kids, all about the kids, because he's a father.

All the power and competence, all the capacity, all the resources of the Creator of the Universe come in the form of a father. He is perfectly able and perfectly relational. He cares about your anxiety and your upset. He empathises with your situation because he's experienced it. He understands the heartache because he's a father. He's *the* Father and he's *your* Father. And he is bigger than anything that you currently face.

Know your place

Jesus explains he is going to prepare a place. In the Jewish wedding ceremony, after betrothal, the bridegroom would go away to prepare a wedding chamber in his father's house. It was done under his father's supervision, and only when his father said everything was ready, would the bridegroom go and collect the bride. She would not know when he was going to arrive – he might be away a long time, and she might begin to feel troubled and anxious and abandoned – but she had to be ready: there would be no warning.

As you wait for the Lord, you could be anxious. But you don't need to be. You can live in the light of the truth that the room is ready. Ready for you. It has your name on it. The bridegroom has gone ahead. Ahead of the bride. Ahead of you. To make the Father's house your home. And now, the bridegroom implores the Bride to live in the reality, to live in the confidence of the future hope and the present reality. And your security is home. You have been included in the family, if it doesn't mess with your head, the bride has become a son.

Jesus is pointing to a new level of knowing God, a new security in God, a new intimacy with God – something that the disciples had not known up to this point – a new identity through him.

> *'Because I live, you also will live. On that day you will realise that I am in my Father, and you are in me, and I am in you.'*
>
> John 14:19, 20

Just as Jesus was secure in knowing who he was and where he was going, he wants his disciples to be. He says there is a place for you. You are *in*, you are *included*, there's plenty of room, if that wasn't so I would have told you. I'm going there, I'm getting it ready for you.

As you lead, there is a truth that the Holy Spirit is wanting you to cling to. There is a place for you in the Father's house. You are not alone, you have not been abandoned, you have not been forgotten or left out. There is a place for you and you are going there. You have a new identity – son. And your call is to live out the culture of the Father's house.

Know where you're going

But then Thomas says 'Lord, we don't know where you are going, so how can we know the way?' (John 14:5). Like Thomas, so often, we aren't sure where home is.

We are a displaced people: nothing on this earth is more misdiagnosed than our homesickness for heaven. Our hearts are anxious and our hearts seek home. That's why you feel grief and anxiety, that's why you feel lost. We want the one we were created for. And we want the place we were made for, the Father's house.

Insecurity is a curse of leadership. I have seen it repeatedly disabling leaders, stunting them in their ability to serve the people that God has called them to love. It brings anxiety and fear, striving and competitiveness. Unclear identity renders leaders impotent in their desire to stoop and serve and love – they don't know who they are and they don't know where they are going.

There is much theoretical security and evident insecurity in leadership in the church of Jesus Christ. So many people whose head knowledge tells them that they have a Father and he has a house, but who don't live as though they believe it. I see leaders jostling for position, churches speaking negatively about one another – I have known jealousy of the role and favour of others.

Often, the church begins to take on the life and character of its leaders. And so the church of Jesus Christ often appears chronically anxious, insanely busy and doesn't witness to a life that anyone who isn't already imprisoned by it would want to imitate or replicate.

In the story of the Prodigal Son Jesus tells of another older brother, a leader, who resides at home but lacks the freedom, joy and identity of a son. His bitter and jealous reactions reek of insecurity. He clearly does not really know the Father or the blessing of being a son. His address is 'The Father's House' but he's not at home there.

Leader, you were made to lead from a place of security and identity and freedom and life that flows from knowing there is a place for you in the Father's house.

I have spent many years as a leader with less security than is healthy, seeking the approval of others and wanting to be liked by all. What I have discovered is that to be liked is overrated, and that aspiring towards the *likes* of others, the *follow* of still more or the *re-tweet* of many, stops me doing the job that God has called me to do. In fact, Jesus calls this a mark of *un*belief.[8] His calling on your life is to believe.

I resolved long ago that I would lay my head on my pillow at night and be accountable firstly to my Father God for what I had done during the day. This might be a good exercise for anyone in leadership to adopt. Reflect on your day, square it with God, sleep the sleep of the righteous and be a conduit of his love.

Leader, if your audience is greater than one, you will lead as if you have something to prove or a position to protect. The truth is that the only position you have of any worth is that of child of God. That cannot be changed, there is no point in protecting it and you have nothing to prove.

You only lead like Jesus if you lead from security.

There is a Father, yours.
He has a house, yours.
It is a home, yours.

This is our security, this is our true destiny, our true address, our true future. Jesus-leaders make an active decision to live between the promise and the fulfilment of that promise with expectation and certainty, with our eyes fixed on our eternal address, not just on our present wanderings. We are citizens of heaven, passing through – and our confidence and our hope arises from who we are in him. And where we live.

Know yourself

You need an environment of security if you are ever to live a life of adventure. So do some mining. Where does your insecurity come from? This is important – you will never lead like Jesus until you do business with this. If you don't know yourself, you can never lead yourself and you will always lead others badly.

---

[8] John 5:44.

Find someone good at excavation and ask them to help you mine. Someone like ...

a spiritual director
a wise mentor
a leadership consultant
a life coach
a FATHER

I have found it to be totally invaluable to have a regular leadership check-up. It reminds me of my wiring: who I am; where I get my energy from; how I operate best; why I find some behaviours difficult. Any number of personality tools can help here – *Myers-Briggs*, *Stengthfinders* and *The Enneagram* – tools that can help you know yourself and your team better.

Stop reading.
Now.
Do some mining.

- Face the experiences that formed you.
- Repent for some.
- Forgive others.
- Recognise your predisposition to certain emotions and dysfunctions and make a plan for the next season which is realistic, based on 'who I am' and not on 'who I wish I was'.

I recommend you do this yearly. Every year. I have found it offers a space for healing and for the recalibration of my heart and gives opportunity to find my way back to the Father's house.

Find an earthly father. Someone who can be a reflection, albeit weakly, of the Father's heart for you.

Find a home

Find an earthly home. Somewhere that you can retreat to – and then advance from. A tribe who will be a counsel of war and a band of brothers. There are many tribes, many families, many places to call home. To be family you must share DNA but you may have different skin. Find a family. The problems of lone wolf leadership are all too obvious. Unaccountable, self-directed leaders become easily lured by the lustre of their own dreams and egos. Not only do they usually end up serving themselves, but they often find themselves alone, paranoid and insecure. None of this gets close to looking like Jesus.

If you really can't find a home, start one! Start one where you are mutually accountable.

> Find a father that draws you to the Father.
> Find a home that calls you to his house.
> Be a father that draws others to the Father.
> Create a home to call others to his house.

FIND COURAGE

Jesus says something more to his disciples. I think this is magnificent. Jesus says, in effect, why don't you trust me and why don't you jump?

> *'Very truly I tell you, whoever believes in me will do the works I have been doing, and they will do even greater things than these . . .'*
>
> John 14:12

Read this again. This is crazy stuff.

Jesus is saying, I'm challenging you and inviting you to live the kingdom now, moment by moment, to do the works I've been doing, and even greater ones than these.

Jesus-leaders are going to do the stuff of Jesus-leadership. They are going to love the unlovely, offer salvation to the lost, heal the sick, demonstrate the kingdom with signs of power and even raise the dead! This will mess with your head, and, if you let it, disturb your life.

But he said it: 'even greater things than these'! Can that be true? Is Jesus really saying that we will look like him and act like him? It may be beyond our current experience, it may compromise our spiritual crumple zone, or it may just make us plain fearful, but it seems to be what Jesus is offering as leadership normality. It is as if he is saying: Remember when I healed the blind man, made the lame man walk, when I offered people salvation and forgiveness of sin, when I raised the dead? Well, you get to do exactly those things … only greater.

Of course the kingdom of God is not all about miraculous signs. They are signs of something greater. Of course great miracles are miracles of justice and inclusion and social action and standing up for the rights of the oppressed – I totally get that – but these greater works are miraculous. I can't see any way around this. In the power of the Holy Spirit leaders are supposed to look like Jesus. And when we begin to look like Jesus, the miraculous happens. We are supposed to see a demonstration of the aliveness of God in our generation. He is doing something – and so are we, and so are we.

To lead in the greater things is to walk in the face of fear; it is to carry courage. Leadership is courage, courage for adventure.

The way of courage is to combat fear. The way in which we choose to walk in courage is to face our fears and do the right thing and not just the expedient thing. So I am totally afraid to pray for healing because I've seen it not work. But I know that I have to. He has called me to *believe* in him.

I am totally afraid to share my faith with my closest non-Christian friends because I fear rejection, but I have to because his love compels me. I am totally afraid to suggest radical change in the church that I lead because I know the pastoral carnage that change can cause, but I suggest it and implement it because I know it's the right thing, it's the Jesus thing, and I do it because Jesus is my example, and I believe in him. And I do it because I have a Father who loves me – and who has a house that is my home that I will one day inhabit fully. Living in the Father's house is my future goal, my permanent address and therefore my present perspective. And the physical action of doing the stuff of the house reminds my soul of who I am and refuses to allow my humanity to take over, deny my identity and have me living less than the leader that I am called to be.

Fear will keep you from your leadership destiny. Believe. And take courage.

Learn to dream

There was a time, way back, when I played with sand, modelled with clay and painted with colour. I drew outside the lines, had imaginary friends and believed that I was Superman and could probably fly. Then I grew up. I rejected all notion of flight. One too many bloody knees helped. I started to reason according to the adult world that I had entered, and stopped much of my dreaming.

But God is a dreamer.
He speaks in dreams.

Jesus sometimes does what appears to be foolish, almost childish. His solution for a blind man was to spit in his eyes. His answer to feeding the multitude was to borrow someone's packed lunch. God encourages imagination and he communicates through more than five senses. He speaks in my gut. He shouts in my emotions. He whispers in my intuitions and he guides in my perceptions. When I embraced leadership, I shut much of this down.

There was a time when I would jump over any wall, vault over any fence and swing over any stream and not think twice about the consequences. 'How hard can it be?' was my mantra. I never worried about the worst case scenario. I attacked every football in the penalty area, not fearing for injury. I had no health and safety concerns and I dressed to be noticed. Then I grew up, and I lost something. I became more fearful, more circumspect and consequently less able to speculate with what I had in my hand.

But God is courageous. In fact, he is the ultimate risk-taker. Jesus' leadership is a study in faith, which so often looks like risk. He leaves the most divine security to step down into what appears to be manmade chaos. He pursues the way of the cross as opposed to the way of the crowd.

The church, should, by definition, be the place of greatest creativity, because God is a dreamer and our biggest adventure. God is courageous. Yet so often the church becomes the organisation of greatest inertia and miniscule innovation. Children are silenced and entertained; teenagers are taught to behave and the place of leadership is reserved for those who stop dreaming and don't risk much.

Is this God's best? Is it leadership?

So many team-building days start awkwardly because leaders of a certain age find it difficult to discover the child that is hidden inside. Of course, activities like building a raft, constructing a tower with toilet rolls, or detangling hands from your colleagues can be irritating and can seem patronising. But rediscovering courage, adventure and fun is more important than you can imagine … if you still can. Only leaders who dream about what they will be able to do will be able to do what they dream of.

The call of the Jesus-leader is to dream with God and then step out with his Spirit. I suggest that the only way to lead afresh, with Jesus' anointing, is to dial back to the imagination and creativity of childhood and the courage and risk of teenagers.

Now, of course the Scriptures are clear about leaving childhood behind and respecting and learning from our elders. I know that, so please don't hear what I'm not saying.

The problem is that some of us left behind our inner child, our inner teenager in such a way that it has disabled our leadership. We are fearful in a way that we don't need to be, limited in a way that we are not supposed to be and have left behind the risk and creativity that are the inheritance of the Father's house.

lack of imagination + risk avoidance = leadership inertia

If we don't allow the Spirit of God to provoke us to dream with God, we will dream with the world and sleepwalk through our leadership journey. Our imaginations, such as they are, will be swamped and corrupted by the philosophy and messaging of a different culture – a culture at odds with the kingdom of God

We will find ourselves discipled by the world.

Retrain the brain

If you never think like a child, or act like a teenager, can you ever really lead like God? Brian is a 50-year-old teenager who is my friend. He also happens to lead one of the best, biggest and most innovative churches I know. He risks. He refuses to stop risking. He will not settle for less than the adventure of life and he will not be restricted by unhelpful rules. He is always looking for a workaround. The environment he creates is not only fun, it is adventuresome. His church is full of radical believers and attracted seekers. In the car park of one of his campuses he has established the most amazing business incubator for young entrepreneurs. He speaks every year on Superbowl weekend at an event he calls 'The Superbowl of Preaching'. Last year over 40,000 people came to the weekend's events, the majority not yet following Jesus. One of his recent sermons was trailered with Brian running with live wolves in the mountains. He loves nothing better than to be on an off-road adventure with his motorbike and some mates, camping out and being free. I think it informs the whole of his life and the philosophy of his ministry, drive fast, have fun, take risks, laugh much, have goals and be family. I think it makes him look a lot like Jesus.

Of course I don't mean you need to 'macho up' your leadership. Your risk may be to stop and stoop and serve, your risk may be to give generously or spend freely, but you have to go after the greater things.

Regress to progress

Science throws up a number of opinions concerning the extent to which the development of the human brain during teenage years increases the potential of a young person to take risks in a way that is lost in later life. There are changes that take place in the forming of the prefrontal cortex and especially in the limbic system, the key part of the brain that controls emotion and behaviour during teenage years. The developmental process appears to create a space for a 'can do' 'why not' 'must do now' attitude, one that is lost later in life. Tomas Paus, Professor of Psychology and Psychiatry at the University of Toronto, however, points out that while neurological images are powerful and informative, images are not causes of behaviour.[9] The brain doesn't just change our experience – experience changes our brain.

Could it be that you can train yourself to think and therefore act in a more courageous way? Can you act in such a way that you begin to think in a different way? Can you trick your brain to embrace a greater imagination, which could increase your ability to lead in a Jesus way? I think this is possible.

How? Well, maybe …

- *Read kids' books to yourself.* Understand how a child learns, how children think.
- *Go to kids' movies* – take some kids with you. What moves their hearts? Ask God to move yours.
- *Life-coach kids:* ask advice from your 5- to 8-year-olds, before they are old enough to give you the kind of answers they think you want to hear.
- *Play to play* and not just to win or achieve or be productive.

---

[9] https://www.ncbi.nlm.nih.gov/pubmed/18979383

- *Step into your creative past*. Pick up a brush, mould some clay, throw some paint, connect with the imagination you used to have and ask God to reconnect you to his mind.

Relearn risk

Two questions to ask yourself:

- What am I afraid of losing?
- What am I trying to prove, and to whom?

Lose

Accumulation always stands against the courageous leadership journey of risk. A movement towards simplicity is powerful in freeing leaders to lead with courage, from the heart. Courageous leadership needs space.

If you have spent your leadership career accumulating kudos, respect, credibility, qualifications, rewards, promotions, members and followers, titles and stuff – you have problems. The collective power of your accumulation can easily suffocate your courageous heart.

But if it does not belong to you – if it is not yours – if you're not collecting any of this, then you can live in a 'no fear' state and you are more readily disposed to courageous decisions. If it is all yours and all you, then you must maintain it, service it and defend it, and you will be predisposed towards protectionism, safety and prudence.

The journey of releasing your heart of courage is a journey that starts with opening your hands.

- Hold a garage sale – real, or virtual. Get rid of possessions that suck time and energy to maintain.
- Take out the huge buffer zones in your budgets, be deeply suspicious of why you hold large reserves and for what reason.

- Give away things as a matter of pattern and with no transactional motive.
- Pass on position, privilege and responsibility to others as soon as you possibly can. Free up your leadership life.

Prove

If Jesus is the way, God is my Father, his house is my home, and this is his adventure, then despite or irrespective of human approvals or rewards I can lead without fear. No pitiful categories of success or failure and no superficial and short-sighted judgments can define me or limit me. God who commissions us to imagine and risk in the adventure of the kingdom is our only judge and he is not only fair, but kind and incredibly good with our failures and redemptive with our mistakes.

So train your brain for an audience of one. Reflect on your day, even throughout the day, whenever you pray, square each encounter and action with God. Be honest with him and with yourself. But you have to prove yourself to no one. And let your heart feel what it means to be courageous.

Speculate

- *Start small.* You do not need to sell everything you have and move to India this week, maybe not ever, but you must learn to put yourself in a space that you can't, by any means of your own, win, without God 'showing up'.
- *Give yourself one challenge a week*, whether it is to share your faith with a stranger or give something away or offer yourself for a role or task that will stretch you. Do it! It will grow your heart and train your brain.
- *Find something to do habitually*, or a place to go or people to hang out with, that frees your heart and opens your mind and helps you lead like Jesus. If you find this difficult, then look for someone who doesn't, and hang out with them. Try 'piggy-backing on someone else's

grace' – in this case risk-taking. Let them be the model and ask them to train you.

Leaders are children of the house. But not so that they might be safe, rather that they might adventure.

Find a Father that draws you to the Father.
Find a home that calls you home.
Be a Father and create a home.

3.

SOURCE

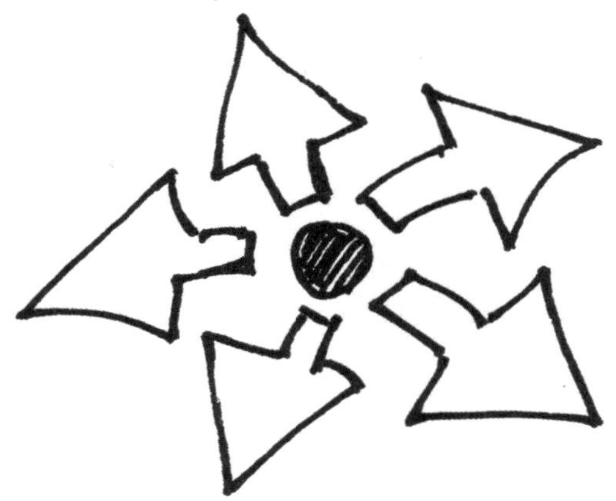

Aim at heaven and you will get earth thrown in. Aim at earth and you will get neither.

CS Lewis

•

'Remain in me, as I also remain in you. No branch can bear fruit by itself; it must remain in the vine. Neither can you bear fruit unless you remain in me.

'I am the vine; you are the branches. If you remain in me and I in you, you will bear much fruit.'

John 15:4–5

'No branch can bear fruit by itself;
it must remain in the vine …'

'If you remain in me and my words
remain in you, ask whatever you
wish, and it will be done for you …'

John 15 /

Not so long ago I found myself in hospital with severe nausea and a lump on my side, feeling totally drained. I started to do some calculations. My grandfather died of stomach cancer at 65. My father died of pancreatic cancer at 65. Maybe my time was up a little earlier?

A barrage of tests revealed that I was fine, I was going to be OK. Unfortunately, the diagnosis of extreme exhaustion and the prescription of immediate rest was given within earshot of my wife.

Shopped!

I took the medicine. I took some time off. I hated doing it, but it was what I needed.

Leadership makes me sick. Often – more often than I would like – leading has made me ill. In truth *I* have made myself ill.

Busyness is a problem for me. I work hard and don't find it easy to switch my head off. There are many weeks when I just don't stop, I preach too much, travel too much, have too many meetings, network too much, write too much, think too much. It's hard, yes, but I also have to admit I enjoy it, I get a buzz from it. In fact I love it, I don't *want* to stop. But then I also want to spend time with my family, get fit, stay fit, go running, play golf, see friends, watch addictive TV mini-series about politics or law firms …

I feel conflicted, if I'm honest. Perhaps it's an addiction.

I have, at times, bought into a lie that soldiering on when I am tired and ill is the noble thing to do. I have felt resentful when others don't. I love my busyness. I am proud of my busyness. And ashamed of my busyness. A few years ago I realised that my usual answer, when someone asked how I was doing, was 'I'm very busy.' I was wearing it like a badge of honour. I'm not sure anyone was all that impressed. But I'm pretty sure I was modelling and fostering a driven culture.

There is an unwritten but universally accepted equation in our culture. It undergirds most leadership practice and appears totally sensible, but in reality it can be anti-kingdom and highly toxic. That equation looks like this:

effort + skills = success

And it is not helping us. In fact, driven leadership is killing the church almost as much as passive leadership is allowing it to die a slow death.

I think Jesus reframes this equation for his leaders. He puts it this way:

abiding + pruning = fruiting

Or, in more detail:

> *'I am the true vine, and my Father is the gardener. He cuts off every branch in me that bears no fruit, while every branch that does bear fruit he prunes so that it will be even more fruitful. You are already clean because of the word I have spoken to you. Remain in me, as I also remain in you. No branch can bear fruit by itself; it must remain in the vine. Neither can you bear fruit unless you remain in me.*
>
> *'I am the vine; you are the branches. If you remain in me and I in you, you will bear much fruit; apart from me you can do nothing. If you do not remain in me, you are like a branch that is thrown away and withers; such branches are picked up, thrown into the fire and burned. If you remain in me and my words remain in you, ask whatever you wish, and it will be done for you. This is to my Father's glory, that you bear much fruit, showing yourselves to be my disciples.*
>
> *'As the Father has loved me, so have I loved you. Now remain in my love. If you keep my commands, you will remain in my love, just as I have kept my Father's commands and remain in his love. I have told you this so that my joy may be in you and that your joy may be complete. My command is this:*

love each other as I have loved you. Greater love has no one than this: to lay down one's life for one's friends. You are my friends if you do what I command. I no longer call you servants, because a servant does not know his master's business. Instead, I have called you friends, for everything that I learned from my Father I have made known to you. You did not choose me, but I chose you and appointed you so that you might go and bear fruit – fruit that will last – and so that whatever you ask in my name the Father will give you. This is my command: Love one another.'

John 15:1–17

Jesus is talking to his disciples and he is concerned for their fruitfulness. Jesus is concerned for *your* fruitfulness. He wants you to bear fruit.

Pause. Get this.
Your leadership is supposed to bear fruit.
You are hardwired for fruitfulness.
And your current activity just might be getting in the way.

Jesus and his disciples have just left the upper room (John 14:31) which is almost certainly at the southwest corner of the old city of Jerusalem. Again, there are no lecture notes, but, as Jesus walks, he talks, he teaches, he disciples. The disciples would have been aware that the vine was a metaphor for Israel, for the people of God. There was a golden vine carved around the portico to the temple – perhaps they walked past it, or could see it. Maybe Jesus picks up a vine trailing over a wall. It probably wouldn't have been in fruit at that time of year, but it might have been in bud or blossom.

Jesus is saying that he is the true vine and his disciples are supposed to bear fruit. Fruit is the thing that is supposed to come out of your life because you belong to him. It's not a static process. You are supposed to bear the fruit of God in this world. Dynamically.

JESUS FRUIT

This fruit looks and tastes like Jesus. We are apprenticed in the life of Jesus, so we're supposed to look like Jesus. What the Father is doing in and through every single leader's life is conforming us to the pattern of Jesus Christ. So this fruit is the transformation of people's lives – this fruit is the year of the Lord's favour, when the broken-hearted get bound up, when sick people get well again. This fruit tastes like Jesus, of grace. It has the taste of righteousness, of love, of truth. It has the same effect as Jesus.

Measurable fruit

This fruit which we are being encouraged to bear is not just fruit. It's more fruit (v. 2). It's much fruit (v. 8) and it is fruit that will last (v. 16). Unpalatable as this may sound, we are supposed to be able to see and measure discipleship. There is supposed to be obvious, measurable, quantifiable, tangible fruit. Not hidden, vague, abstract fruit.

Abundant fruit

We are supposed to desire more of it. We're supposed to be hungry for fruit. Desperate for the fruit of the kingdom of God.

This is a hugely challenging concept if, like me, you grew up in a culture where the acceptable Christian thing was to be uber-modest and respectfully conservative, not to grab at things, not to expect big things, and not to put our heads above the parapet. To hunger or even be greedy for fruit, kingdom fruit, doesn't appear to be very British. To my shame, often I have been cynical about and critical of those who appeared desperate for more of the kingdom.

Who is wrong in this? Probably me.

I was standing near the front at a large Pentecostal conference in the middle of an epic worship fest and I was not in a good place. There was a shaking and a quaking and a flag-waving that was seriously disturbing me. The floor was covered with bodies and those that were still standing were sweating profusely as the volume and intensity of the praise band reached crescendo. My cynical head firmly screwed on, I worked out where people could put their flags … and determined not to respond to the instructions to 'dance, dance, everybody dance'. We were one *shofar* away from an old-time revival. As I stood there, very distinctly, the Holy Spirit said to me 'Who's the saddo here – is it the flag-wavers full of the joy of the Lord, abandoned in praise, or is it the cynic standing in judgment?'

Now don't get me wrong, I'm still not overly keen on flags. And you can blow a *shofar* if you like – just do it a long way away. But increasingly I want the joyful abundant fruit of the kingdom of God. And I don't care really what it looks like for me to get it.

Jesus is ALIVE. And his kingdom is at hand and all things are possible! Jesus says, I want you to have more fruit, I want you to have much fruit, and I want that fruit to last. And I want that fruit to be tasty, and fruity. I don't want it to be joyless and miserable and shrivelled up and smelling of condemnation. I want you to bear fruit.

Love joy peace patience goodness kindness faithfulness self-control. The fruit of the Holy Spirit. The fruit of the leadership of Jesus.

Do you want more? Do you want more of God? Because he always has more for you.

Lasting fruit

It is fruit that will last. It will last and be passed on, and on, and on.

Jesus didn't count '12 – 24 – 36 – 48'. He counted 12 – 72 – 3000[10] – and eventually 50%. Of the world. The implication in

[10] Luke 9:1–6; Luke 10:1–20; Acts 2:41.

the Parable of the Sower is that multiplication is the normative expectation of the kingdom. The numbers are mind-frying. Read it again: Mark 4:3–20; 8, 20.

30 times
60 times
100 times

Can you imagine hundredfold growth? Growth in wisdom, growth in influence, growth in compassion, growth in resources, growth in leadership, growth in pioneering?

Not possible? Yet somehow the disciples seem to work out this equation in their leadership lives and bear fruit on just this kind of scale.

And again, the story of the early church, given to us by doctor Luke, is a story of multiplication. Luke uses two Greek words to describe the growth of the church at that time. In the early chapters he uses the word *prosetethe* (Acts 2:41) to describe the result of the pouring out of the Holy Spirit at Pentecost. The Lord 'added' to their number.[11] He is describing a one-off event of additional growth. But after the raising up of leaders to serve the fledgling church (Acts 6:1, 7), and then again during persecution and after the freeing of Peter from jail (Acts 12:24) Luke uses the Greek word *plethynei* which on both occasions is translated 'multiply'. The activity of the Holy Spirit which we first saw drawing people to faith through one-off events and experience and the leadership of the few has, within a few chapters, become something multi-faceted, a leadership lifestyle shared by many, a cultural movement. Our heritage is discipleship multiplication. So why do most of our models aspire to events-based growth, to one-off addition?

Multiplication is the holy grail of leadership. If I can only add to but can't multiply something, or myself, the effort in

[11] This word *prosetethe*, or added, is used several other times before the appointing of leaders in Acts (2:47, 5:14) but also at least once afterwards (11:21) so we can't draw too hard a rule from this observation.

my leadership is seriously limited, one-dimensional, one-generational and incredibly vulnerable. But if I (or rather, the Lord) can multiply something – or, preferably, someone – then what I am doing can become scalable and can even perhaps become a movement. The potential for exponential fruit is huge.

This is leadership.

THE SECRET OF FRUITFULNESS

Of course this line of argument is open to the challenge that we are obsessed with numbers and driven by this kind of success. Is it possible to hold in tension the need to see the fruit of the kingdom of God, and for that not always to be immediate or numerical? Of course. That there needs to be fruit is a given. And of course we long to see that love, joy, patience and kindness growing in others – in many others – that is our calling. When that fruit comes and how it comes are variables. Sometimes I have found myself frustrated in ministry because the fruit of the kingdom of God does not come according to my timing.

Jimmy is an understated, wise, young leader. He is one of the most fruitful young men I know; in a quiet way he leads other young people to Jesus, like Jesus. But there was a time when I couldn't have written this. Jimmy was one of my early apprentices. He had incredible potential. He was incredibly frustrating. It appeared to me almost as if he was determined to undermine his own future. Jimmy and I had an interesting relationship. He was one of my spiritual children but he was the one I was always telling off. I didn't see the fruit that I was expecting and wasn't sure when I would. It took Jimmy a few years of getting his stuff in order, to trace his circle, draw his line and plant his stake. Learning how to live as part of the family with a place in the Father's house, he is now bearing much fruit – I'm looking forward to abundant fruit. We now call Jimmy 'James'. James is growing up secure and increasingly able to speculate for the kingdom.

Fruit is God's business and fruit comes in God's way on God's clock. But it will come. For James the story hasn't ended. Your story still has a way to go and there are more chapters to be written.

ABIDE

Jesus here is interested in more than just the fruit. He is concerned with the process by which fruit comes. There is only one way. Jesus says, fruitfulness is on me … *only*. It is all about relationship with me, I need you to learn to remain with me, in me. Abide.

Nine times in this short section Jesus uses the word '*meno*', which means 'remain' or 'abide'.

Abide
Abide
Abide
Abide
Abide
Abide
Abide
Abide
Abide

Get the message? Jesus is saying that the key to fruitfulness, the key to success in leadership, the heart of walking with him, being and modelling discipleship, is that we learn to abide.

Def…

abide /ə'bʌɪd : continue without fading or being lost
Old English ābīdan, 'wait'

Def…

meno. μὲνω : remain, to abide, or to stay

For this enigmatic thing called leadership, there is a core, a key, a prime mover. There is an inner part and if it isn't working the outer part will never happen.

Remain.

Abide.

The inner part is all about intimacy, the inner part is all about cooperation with the Godhead. It's not about what you are doing – it's about your participation in what God is doing in you.

Jesus said, 'I no longer call you servants … but I have called you friends, and all that I have heard from my Father I have made known to you' (John 15:15). He doesn't treat us like servants, sending us off to do isolated tasks – he invites us to join the table, he invites us in on the plan, in the same way that God shared his plans with Abraham. To cooperate is better than to operate.

You don't do anything without him.

Jesus says, 'Remain in me.'

The fruit of your life is dependent on the root of your life. Here's the thing I want you to understand – if the root of your life is Jesus, and Jesus is the King of Kings and the Lord of Lords, and Jesus is the living Word of God, and Jesus is the Maker, the Owner and the Sustainer of the world, if Jesus is the Lord of all things – then the resources of your life *have* to be abundant. And the adventure of your life *has* to be exciting. And the power of your life *has* to be incredible. And the leadership of your life *has* to be wise. Because it is the leadership of Jesus. Because it is this relationship that has become the source of every other relationship.

If you want fruit, then the reality and quality of this relationship is *everything*. There is *one* thing you have to do:

You must remain.

You want fruit? Don't go after fruit. Go after Jesus. Because he is the fruitful one.

Prioritise abiding above any other life practice. The activity that Jesus wants you to engage in is always borne out of engagement with Jesus.

Initially just for you.

You and Jesus.

Unless you abide, there will be no fruit!

I was coaching a younger leader recently who told me that he felt that his relationship with Jesus so often looked like an upside down iceberg. As an extreme extrovert and church leader he spent time with Jesus for everybody else. Everything he learned he would use to preach or coach or pastor others. The attitude was noble but counterproductive and would soon lead to dryness and fruitlessness. I felt convicted because so often that has been me. I pray for other people, with other people about other people. But it is rarely just me and Jesus. I read for preparation for other people but not often for edification for my soul. Serving God can so often become the biggest hindrance to abiding, which, ironically, ends up killing that service.

Stop leading for Jesus and start looking at Jesus. *Then* you'll lead like Jesus.

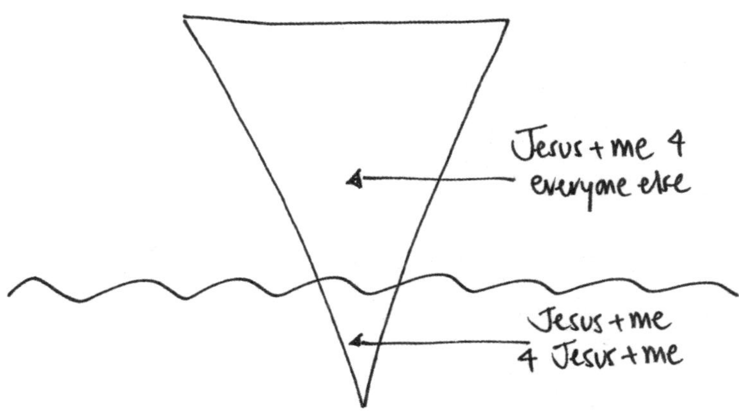

Abide – just you and Jesus.

Jesus as Friend.
Jesus as Saviour.
Jesus as Lord.

Know him, trust him, obey him.

It takes time.

Worship

Eugene Peterson describes worship as 'the strategy by which we interrupt our preoccupation with ourselves and attend to the presence of God'.[12] Interrupt yourself. Go on. Spend regular time just soaking in the presence of Jesus. Ask him

---

12 Eugene Peterson, *Leap Over a Wall: Earthy Spirituality for Everyday Christians* (HarperSanFrancisco, 2002).

to help you switch off your inner agendas and diary-anxiety and abide. I have discovered that thankfulness is the door to intimacy: start by just telling him how grateful you are and allow him to remind you who he is and what he is doing and rediscover you.

Prayer

Prayer is the dynamic practice wherein we posture ourselves towards the heart of God and attempt to catch it. Prayer is the place where we allow him to remind us of reality. We turn off the noise of the world and recalibrate ourselves to the ground bass of heaven. Prayer and worship are the activities whereby we waste our life on Jesus. Like Mary of Bethany before us we break open our jar of nard and lavish our affection and devotion on Jesus because he is worth it all. Worship, if you allow it, will reframe your leadership life.

Scripture

Reading the word is the discipline of anchoring our lives and our leadership in the plans and purposes of God. It is a constant invitation to 'Speak, Lord, for your servant is listening.'[13] It encourages the practice of making what God has said, and is saying, the foundational authority of our lives. Never has the practice of reading and applying the word of God been more important. We are constantly bombarded by noise, by things good and not so good, incessantly demanding our attention, encouraging us to pay attention to every other opinion, every other authority. Reading the word – allowing it to percolate in our minds and marinade our souls – gives perspective to our leadership.

Amongst other practices such as solitude (really hard for me) silence (also) fasting (same). These things help us stay cemented in Jesus. He in us, us in him.

---

[13] 1 Samuel 3:9.

There are many ways to worship and pray and read. Find the one that is right for you at each stage you are at. Don't ever be restricted by another's pattern and certainly never be condemned by anyone else's style. You must abide, and, because of your wiring and your stage of life and, your calling, your abiding will look different from mine.

Whatever your thing is, you will need to develop habits that help you do it. And you will need to stick at it.

I have some pretty weird friends. One of the strangest is the guy I run with. When I say 'run', I mean once a week I run with him. He runs every day. As I write he is celebrating an anniversary: he has run every day, currently at least four miles every day, for the past 2,345 days. He has run through the foulest of winters and the hottest of summers, on high days and holidays, with broken legs and pulled muscles. To say he has a habit in his life would be a significant understatement. What is clear, though, is that there is an ease and a rhythm and almost a beauty to his run. His cadence is unhindered, and his fitness is unquestionable.

I want some of what he has. Not all! Much of it is a little strange. But the focus, the discipline, the passion, the fluidity and the fitness – I want that for my leadership and I covet the fruit that I know comes through it.

Get obsessed with the presence of God – do whatever you can to abide.

The secret to the fruitfulness of your leadership is your singular ability to abide, but the key to your abiding lies in the habits you form and practice in your life to enable you to abide. Of course the development of habits is dependent on favourable environments.

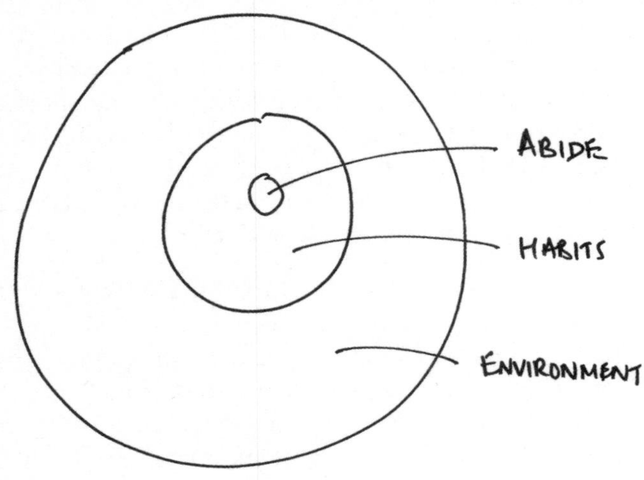

What does it look like for you to abide?
What habits do you need to grow for abiding to occur?
How do you need to change your environment to enable these habits?

The environment we created in our permanent 24-7 Prayer room has been fertile ground for the birthing of many kingdom dreams and much fruitfulness. Amongst a number of ministry calls and recommitments we have also seen a number of entrepreneurial business ventures launched, Muddy Pearl's publishing house prominent amongst them.

The habitual rhythms we have created as a church family include shared morning Bible reading and shared daily gathering for devotions. We encourage an interruption at midday all across our city to say the Lord's prayer and a challenge to examine ourselves at night – and all this has led to a new depth of abiding that is bearing fruit.

Of course you don't need to adopt our habits. But you will need some of your own if you are to abide, if you are to be fruitful.

OF GRACE JUNKIES AND TRUTH MONKEYS

There are two different and maybe opposite reactions to the call to abide. According to your personality and experience, you will hear this differently. And it will disable you in bearing fruit if you hear it wrongly.

There is one type of leader who, when reading this, will say to themselves: 'Hey man, all I've got to do is remain. All I've got to do is abide. All I got to do is just hang out with God.' These are the Grace Junkies.

The other group, absolutely diametrically opposed, I call the 'Truth Monkeys'. They say, 'The Word said remain. The Greek word is *meno*. It means to endure, to abide. It means to dwell and has a sense of will or perseverance and I'm going to do it and make it happen.' And they do, but it's all in their own strength.

Our hope is in a tension. A tension between truth and grace. Not one or the other, but *both-and*, not some kind of unsatisfactory balance in the middle. To abide as a leader you are going to need both: extreme grace *and* extreme perseverance. Jesus doesn't offer the choice between being the Good Samaritan who serves his neighbour in love and the devotion of Mary who anoints Jesus' feet – he calls for both. You get to just remain, you get to just abide, but you've got to persevere. What Jesus is saying is that abiding is about discipline and dependence.

So many leaders, and consequently our teams, are obsessed with dependence and forget about discipline. Or we are obsessed with discipline and forget about dependence. We either have all the form but no life, or all the life but no form. And neither will bear any fruit. Or the fruit that is borne is shrivelled because we bore it ourselves, in our own strength.

TRUTH MONKEYS

Jesus says 'my Father is the gardener and he cuts off every branch that does not bear fruit' (v. 1). Which sounds a bit harsh doesn't it? However 'to cut off' is just one translation of the Greek word '*areo*'. In truth there are four possible translations of that word. One of them means to 'remove or cut off', but three refer to lifting or raising up. It would make some sense to read this as 'he lifts' because that is what a good vinedresser does. He lifts and ties up an unfruitful branch to allow air and light to reach it, so that it can develop more strongly the next season, and also to prevent it from putting down roots.[14]

My Father is the gardener. He is the one whose whole reason and objective for being in the garden is that you and I bear fruit. He's the one whose desire is that we get conformed to the person of Jesus so that our fruit looks like Jesus. You and I get to be and produce beautiful, refreshing and life-bringing wine of the kingdom. That is what it is all about.

He wants to lift you. And bring you into the light, to breathe on you and for you to receive his Spirit. He wants to heal you and produce fruit with your life. You can't do it. He can. Your job is to receive his lifting. It's about dependence. It's *all* about dependence. Fruitful discipleship is not about the absence of sin or the adherence to a doctrine. It's all about the presence of Jesus, the lifting presence of God. This is huge.

See, I grew up thinking that the job specification for a good Christian life was all about a stack of things that you didn't do or watch or buy. Being a Christian for many of us was about adhering to a gospel of not-sinning-very-much. Despite a whole programme of grace rehabilitation these things stick – they stick in my leadership style.

The only way to lead in the kingdom is to stop trying to lead in the kingdom.

---

[14] However, it is undeniable that one sense of the word must be that those who don't abide in the Lord will eventually wither and be thrown away and gathered up and thrown into the fire (John 15:6), and this refers back to warnings to Israel and the destruction of the vineyard throughout the Old Testament (Isaiah 5:5–7; Jeremiah 5:10; 12:10; Hosea 2:12; Amos 4:9).

The *one thing* you have got to do is to learn to abide. The one way that you can learn to abide is to be full of the Holy Spirit of Jesus. This passage is bookended by Jesus' most in-depth teaching on the Holy Spirit: the Spirit of Jesus and the Spirit of Truth. The answer to fruitfulness is not that you battle and strive, it is not that you spend your life trying not to sin. Because that will kill you. And it will kill the God-life in you and it will hurt everyone else around you who will get hit by the shrapnel of you trying not to sin. Abiding means that you get to live by the Spirit, and, when you live by the Spirit, the fruit of the Spirit begins to grow in you, and you get to abide.

Jesus said it is your abiding that will do the fruiting. But we become known for our striving and our driving and our busyness and our productivity. The Protestant work ethic sometimes appears to be more our gospel than the grace-soaked way of Jesus. Truth Monkeys, if any of this is in any way a description of your leadership, address it fast. Otherwise, all you will model is a life that no one can attain and no one wants, and a witness to a god who isn't, rather than the God who is. It's that big.

The way in is the way on

As I travel and speak, I meet many leaders who began in leadership with great dreams and great grace, but slowly and certainly their dreams were crushed and their vision was compromised. They came in on a tidal wave of grace knowing their weaknesses and accepting his strength. Knowing his forgiveness and depending on his power. But as they got busy and purposeful they laid aside the principle of abiding, and lost the wonder of grace. Their dreams were forgotten and amidst the striving and driving and settling they began to live only truth. It is hard to write because I see the faces of some of my friends. It is so common. Jesus said *abide*.

Slow down, go easy on yourself, take a breath, take a break and chase Jesus. He's easy caught! Find a space – seek his face – and you will rediscover grace.

> *Are you tired? Worn out? Burned out on religion? Come to me. Get away with me and you'll recover your life. I'll show you how to take a real rest. Walk with me and work with me – watch how I do it. Learn the unforced rhythms of grace. I won't lay anything heavy or ill-fitting on you. Keep company with me and you'll learn to live freely and lightly.*
>
> Matthew 11:28–30 (The Message)

As long as your address is 'The Vine' you will bear fruit. So stop striving and driving and start abiding.

Get a dog.

We did, a spaniel. Ash brings much joy and mischief to the Martin house but she brings one thing above anything else. The discipline of the walk. Alone. The hill, the dawn, the silence. God and I. Every day. No phone, no notebook, just me and God … and Ash.

Truth monkeys: get a dog. And drop some stuff – stop some activity – lose some responsibility. The load you carry is more than you are supposed to carry. That's why you feel so tired.

Imagine there are four bags, labelled:

'God's', 'Somebody Else's', 'Nobody's', 'Mine'.

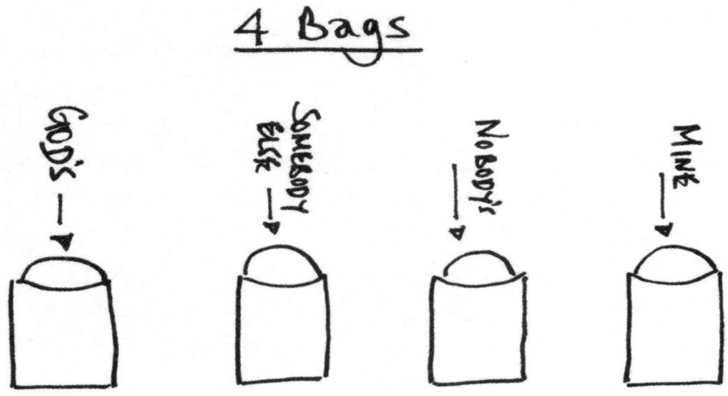

Now empty out your own bag and look at everything that you have been carrying. Ask three questions:

- What is someone else's to carry? Give it away.
- What is God's to carry? Offer it up to him.
- What is no one's to carry? Stop it now.

Now pick up your bag and carry it well, Truth Monkey.

GRACE JUNKIES

If the way in which you do kingdom leadership is a little more 'hey man just abide.' Then listen carefully:

The way to lead in the kingdom of God is to start trying to lead in the kingdom of God. Start with yourself.

See, it is all about discipline. There are things that you can't do that only God can do. But there are things that you must do. There is God's part and there is your part and your job is to do your part!

At least 75% of the members of the church I have the privilege to lead are under the age of thirty. We are full of Grace Junkies. Grace Junkies are great to lead but generally make hesitant leaders. We are always battling with a culture of entitlement and a hesitation to take responsibility. Sometimes we are so laid back we are in danger of falling over. But we have to take our place and play our part. Lead ourselves and lead others, and, as Paul said, 'take hold of that for which Christ Jesus took hold of [us]' (Philippians 3:12).

You can remain, you can devote, you can love, you can serve. You can abide. And you must. If you want to see fruit.

What does that look like? If you're going to live this Christian life, if you're going to pursue discipline, you've got to want instruction. You've got to eagerly desire instruction – and not avoid it.

Jesus reminds his disciples:

'You are already clean because of the word I have spoken to you.'

John 15:3

It is his words that make them clean – it is Jesus' words that are going to continue to make us clean. Jesus' words must remain in us if we are to remain at all! When you root yourself in the vine, when you pursue him, he comes, not as a silent visitor – he comes as an authoritative guest. He comes as one who has things to say about your life. He comes as one who has correction to bring. He has truth that he wants to speak. He has a light that he wants to shine. He has commands that are to be obeyed. You can't have abiding without this kind of obedience. True freedom and perfect grace come under authority not outside of it.

Have you ever read the Bible cover to cover?

Do it! His book is a love letter to you, it's the guide for your life, it's the annals of the history of God. If you want to be a leader in the kingdom of God, you have got to let the word of God dwell in you, which means you've got to read it. You've got to read it daily. You breathe every day. You eat every day. You relate to people every day. So read – eat – breathe – relate to God. Daily.

If you are predisposed to be a Grace Junkie, the path to fruitfulness is a road that goes through the valley of discipline and devotion. 'If you keep my commands, you will remain in my love' (John 15:10).

Buy a Bible. I try to every year; wide margin. And buy some pens, nice ones. And fill your margins with the word of God to you. I recently inherited my father's first King James, leather bound, wide margin Bible. It has his notes in the margins and on many pages he has inscribed FM, 'for me'. Do it.

You've got to desire intervention as well. Pruning. The word here, *katherai,* can refer to pruning, cleansing, and to lifting up. When the grapes get too heavy and fall onto the ground, they get dirty and bruised, damaged, and are no use for wine. So the vinedresser takes the grapes and ties them up so they are lifted up off the ground, ready to be washed clean, so that they might bear fruit. There is also a process of cleansing, a removal of suckers or insects or dirt. And there is actual pruning – a painful process, I imagine. The gardener lifts up, and cleanses, but he also prunes.

If you are going to bear more fruit, abundant fruit, fruit that will last, he's going to have to change some things in your life. He may have to challenge some things, shake some things, disturb some things. Cut some things out, anything that is incompatible with abiding, anything that will disable fruiting. Any appetite that distracts from your calling; any ambition that is not Jesus' ambition for you; any approval that you live for that is not the Father's – he wants to cut out.

The effectiveness of leadership is so often limited by an unwillingness to engage with the disturbance that comes when the Saviour of the world wants to prune us. Years and years of ministry bearing only limited fruit, never quite seeing what could have been, stem from saying 'no' to the knife. It's never too late to have a cut.

Leader, that's really important to hear. You see, it's relatively easy to see the need for pruning when you are young in your leadership journey, but when you have done some miles and fought some battles and had some victories, when you are set in your ways, you are perhaps not so open to his cut.

Just as you have to let him lift you, you need to allow him to prune you. However old you are, however good you are. Who is helping you to see the need for pruning? Who do you trust? Who is going to challenge you?

I have been deeply convicted by the Spirit recently about my lack of courage in witnessing to my faith. When I say the Spirit convicted me, it was the Spirit through my wife, who said 'you really need some new stories'. So I am letting him cut me, humble me, grow me. I want to be fruitful. I have challenged myself to have one story of boldness every week – so far it's working.

'Father, 'cos I want to be fruitful I want to be a disciple, I'm open to your blade, I'm open to that scalpel of the word of God, I'm open to your discipline, I'm open to your changing things in my life, I'm open to the disturbance that means I'm going to have to alter to your pattern because I want fruit.'

'If you will here stop and ask yourself why you are not as pious as the early Christians were, your own heart will tell you that it is neither through ignorance nor inability, but purely because you never thoroughly intended it.'

WILLIAM LAW (a serious call to a devout and holy life)

What do you need to change?
What do you need to start?
What do you need to stop?

The Father wants to love you by lifting and pruning. He is predisposed to desire and work for fruitfulness in your leadership. But it only comes one way.

Meno. Abide.

4.

SCHOOL

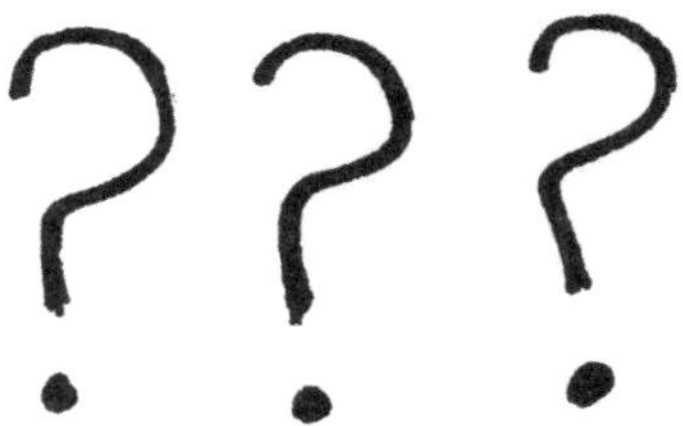

Who is a wise man? He who learns of all men.

The Talmud

•

Learn from yesterday, live for today, hope for tomorrow – the important thing is not to stop questioning.

Albert Einstein

•

'All this I have told you so that you will not fall away. They will put you out of the synagogue; in fact, the time is coming when anyone who kills you will think they are offering a service to God. They will do such things because they have not known the Father or me. I have told you this, so that when their time comes

you will remember that I warned you about them. I did not tell you this from the beginning because I was with you . . .'

John 16:1–4

•

'I have told you these things, so that in me you may have peace. In this world you will have trouble. But take heart! I have overcome the world.'

John 16:33

'The problem is you have no persecution.'

I had been venting frustration at the lack of exponential growth in the church in Britain when my friend, an Indian pastor said this. He went on to challenge me: 'You haven't learned the joy of enduring, of complete faith and of real community because you have never had to.'

This line of argument is hard to hear. I want to … and I really don't.

If you were to do an analysis of growth and health in the church worldwide, if you could measure spiritual maturity in any way, you would likely find spikes in your graphs, showing burgeoning numerical growth and mesmerizing testimony around, after and in, significant persecution.

Take China, 1953. When the church experienced terrible repression and persecution under the Communist regime and all foreign missionaries were expelled. The church grew rapidly underground, initially, and is now growing very much above ground. It is estimated that today there are over 100 million followers of Jesus in that previously closed country.

Take Nepal, 1990. A Hindu nation, closed to Christians – and against the fiercest of opposition, the church has become currently possibly the fastest-growing church on the planet, even in the wake of the terrible earthquake of 2015.

Take Baghdad, 2016, where even amongst the shrapnel and bombs of conflict, and in the shadow of ISIS, the church is flourishing.

Where there is persecution, there you will find life and multiplication growth.

ANTIFRAGILE

The writer and risk analyst, Nassim Nicholas Taleb, coined the phrase 'antifragile'[15] to describe certain things which, like bindweed and the human body, seem to gain from disorder: the

---

15 Nassim Nicholas Taleb, *Antifragile: Things that gain from disorder* (Penguin, 2012).

more pressure or trauma you place upon them, the more they strengthen, grow and prosper. One of the subjects Taleb could have written about is the church.

The church is antifragile. It is flexible and nubile, it flourishes in the harshest of environments and grows under the greatest difficulty and persecution. And leadership, Jesus-leadership, is antifragile.

> *'If the world hates you, keep in mind that it hated me first.'*
>
> John 15:18

Now there's a verse that is not often tattooed on the right forearm of hipster Christian leaders.

> *'They will put you out of the synagogue; in fact, the time is coming when anyone who kills you will think they are offering a service to God.'*
>
> John 16:2

Jesus is speaking to his leaders and warns them of trouble ahead, not so they can run away from it or duck out, but so that they can stand and grow through it. He knows that the very same leaders he is talking to – if they lead for him, like him – will face persecution. He knows because he will face it first.

Most of them will be killed for what they are leading. They will see their brothers and sisters dipped in tar and lit up as torches for emperors' parties and others ripped apart by wild animals for the entertainment of the crowds. They will lead a people who will be passed over, despised, rejected and imprisoned under their leadership.

On their watch.

Jesus also knows that this most under-pressure, persecuted movement will be the body through which the gospel of grace is communicated and the kingdom of God advances. And it will grow exponentially. This tiny persecuted minority will grow under pressure until, within three centuries, 50% of the known world are following Jesus. Not despite, but *because* of the pressure they will face.

Antifragile.

It is still true. It is in places of persecution and oppression that you will find antifragile leaders, leaders who prosper under pressure. When things are hard, there is a perspective that leads to flourishing.

Your trials will grow you.

They may even bless you!

But you have to want to grow. And whether your testing and trial takes the form of criticism and misunderstanding from your friends, colleagues or church, or whether it is imprisonment and even death, you have an opportunity to grow in it every day. It's a choice.

Every day is a school day

When Niki and I gather emerging leaders in our house to teach and input into their lives, one of the challenges we give them is to articulate the five rules of life they hope to live by. At least one person in every cohort has suggested the life rule that 'every day is a school day.' Every day of my leadership life will be a day in which I learn. It's a vital and noble ambition. But I'm not sure that when my emerging leaders form these grand ambitions, they think about trouble and persecution as being the schoolroom and the exam theatre for that rule. And I'm not sure that I have been consciously training them to be antifragile. Yet that's what Jesus is doing.

Jesus is talking to his disciples about growing and maturing in a context and culture that might appear to be hostile. He starts by warning them, if you are going to lead my way, the world is going to hate you (John 15:18, 20) and ends by saying, 'In this world you will have trouble.' (16:33). The word he uses is *thlipsis*, which means 'gut-wrenching heartache.' Encouraging stuff! Sandwiched between these two encouragements, Jesus fills in with examples: they will put you out of the synagogue, they will try to kill you, they will ostracise you and even believe that in taking your life they have done a good thing.

Jesus warns us to expect trouble. And that trouble will be real. But he also says that you can grow, and you will have joy as you grow.

> *'Blessed are those who are persecuted*
> *because of righteousness,*
> *for theirs is the kingdom of heaven.*
>
> *'Blessed are you when people insult you, persecute you and falsely say all kinds of evil against you because of me. Rejoice and be glad, because great is your reward in heaven, for in the same way they persecuted the prophets who were before you.'*
>
> Matthew 5:10–12

Choose to grow

I don't like pain.
Or sacrifice.
Or cost.

I look for comfort and the surety of the known. Yet the call I embraced when I said 'Yes' to Jesus and to leadership was to deny self, to take up my cross and follow him.

Disciples grow, and leaders grow. The word translated 'disciple' is the Greek word *mathetes,* which means 'learner'. For any disciple every day is a school day. You grow by learning in all circumstances. The leadership laboratory is no ivory tower experience. It is, at its best, an experiential training school in the raw stuff of life.

I am not wishing in any way at all to underestimate or trivialise the pain and suffering that we will all go through, the trials we will face, or the opposition that we will encounter. As I write this, Christian leaders are not only facing opposition but in parts of our world are having their heads cut off for following Jesus and leading his people. Leadership is difficult. You will have '*thlipsis*'.

What I am trying to say is that there is a perspective that we can have, a posture that we can adopt, a choice that we can make: we can choose to grow under pressure, and hope for joy.

Jesus implies that you will have trouble. Expect it! If you are really following Jesus, leading like Jesus, you will have the same impact as Jesus had, positively and negatively. You will bless people, see people's lives transformed and you will experience trouble, the kind of trouble that Jesus had. You will find people 'of peace', who want to help and enable what you are called to, who serve you and bless you and follow you, but you will find people of conflict who oppose you. They may not kill you but they may well undermine you, slander you and seek to destroy your leadership. Expect it. Expect testing and learn from it.

Can you? Of course. If every day is a school day, you can learn from it all. In fact, perhaps you can redeem the trouble to become joy, by growing in it, *because* of it rather than despite it.

CRITIQUE, CONFLICT AND COUNSEL

The law of the 1%

As you lead, you will be criticised. Any leader offering to be a guide, offering to speak truth and life, sticks their head above the parapet of the mundane, the *status quo ante* and the comfort of the known. That will always provoke an attack from the fearful and the comfortable. Expect it. And learn from it.

In every critique, however harsh or selfish, there will be truth. There is always at least 1% that is fair and can be learned from. Embrace the law of 1%. It will grow you. I have discovered growth opportunities in all kinds of criticism. When I have been brave enough to stand in the full glare of critique, and have not retreated to a well-defended, unassailable, fortified position of my own correctness, I have grown.

Whether I was moving our church's location (again) or changing its name, whether we were introducing a fresh vision, a radical structure, or a new team member, or whether I was teaching some unfamiliar ancient value, I have faced trouble. Often from within the family. I can honestly say that every time I refused to close down and protect my heart, I have learned. I have learned more about God, more about me and more about leadership and have made better decisions.

Actively look out for the 1% and embrace it.

(In my case it is almost always more than 1%.)

I leave a considerable amount of room in my leadership for critique. I have married people and called them the wrong name in the wedding service. I have smashed someone's head whilst baptising them in the pool, filling the tank with blood. More significantly, I have let people down. I have over-promised and under-delivered. I have moved too fast, changed too much, taken my stand over the wrong issues and attempted to die on the wrong hills. Some of these have had devastatingly negative impacts on people I love. But I have learned, and I have grown.

Every day is a school day.

Seek feedback

I have a big ambition. I want to be the best me I can be: I want to be more able to fulfil the call that the Lord has placed on my life. I want to stand before Jesus face to face, be satisfied and be spent. But I need help. I am in no way the finished article. I need help. So I seek feedback. It is uncomfortable but if I want to grow into the fullness of my leadership, I need feedback. So do you. Ask people: 'tell me what you see'. What does it look like to be the other side of me?

Counsel and opinion

Recognise the difference between counsel and opinion. Not so that you can embrace counsel and reject opinion, but rather so that you can allow it to have the weight that it deserves as you grow.

Wise counsel comes from the heart of God; it is wisdom mediated by his children, set on getting God's way, and for the building up of his people. It is marked by love and to be coveted. Whatever the governance structure of your church or organisation, you will be a weaker leader if you never seek the mind and counsel of the many and the few.

After many years in church leadership and observing various models, I am increasingly convinced that you will not grow a healthy organisation without a fair balance of three biblical governance styles: Episcopal, Presbyterian and Congregational.

- As a leader you need to lead: *It's on you.* You are the equivalent of an Episcopal bishop.
- As a leader you need a team of leaders: *It's on us.* We are the Presbyterian team.
- As leaders we need the wisdom of God mediated by the people of God: *It's on all of us.* We are the Congregation, the gathered people of God.

Niki and I, over years of ministry, have had the privilege of leading teams who bring counsel, and church meetings that offer counsel, but have supplemented that with a support group who are encouraged not only to pray for us but to speak counsel into our lives, the life of our family and our ministry. We would not be where we are today without counsel. They hold opinions, but they do so with wisdom, perspective and responsibility.

Those who simply voice opinions sometimes seem to want to express a view and be noticed. Remember, constructive criticism never flows from the heart of a person bent on destruction. Remember, conviction is the regular tool of the Holy Spirit and provokes life, but condemnation comes from another place and encourages death. Please respect it when your people think hard. When they have views. When they engage their minds, and care enough about the things of God to wrestle with the right approach for the people of God. But check motive and agenda and source. As a leader, you would be wise to have zero tolerance for irresponsible opinion-holders and you would covet wise counsel-givers. Surround yourself with wise counsel. Protect yourself from irresponsible opinion.

There is huge value in the opinion of the crowd. You can test what will work and what is likely to crash and burn, but your inner team must be populated with wise counsellors. Maybe this is just for me, but I have discovered that my leadership does not flourish with a team who are high on opinion and low on counsel. It just makes me dysfunctionally defensive. I have no one in my close team who doesn't love the vision God has given, who doesn't support Niki and I in that vision, and who doesn't bring serious counsel to the table. But maybe that's just my heart: you need to care for yours, grow yours!

The wisdom of conflict. 'Yes' people are 'No' people

Don't hear what I'm not saying. I'm not saying, 'Surround yourself with "yes" people.' Any leader that sets up their leadership team to be an echo chamber is a leader who doesn't want to grow. Don't surround yourself with people who just agree with you. You just set yourself up for fragile leadership.

The child psychologist, Jean Piaget, saw conflict as a crucial component of growth and development. Battling with peers grows you. Equally a predisposition in our culture to over-protective parenting will stunt growth. Even as an adult, having conflict with those around you schools you, refines your ideas, challenges the way that you look at the world. The day you shut down conflict is the day you cease to grow.

What you need is counsel that brings conflict.

I was recently privileged to sit in on a conversation with the owner of one of the most successful private equity firms in the world as he described the wisdom of conflict.

He set out the process of acquiring a failing company and talked about many months of rigorous due diligence by the purchasing team. At the climax of the purchasing process, they then bring in a completely new team called a 'red team' whose sole job is to undermine the basis of confidence in the purchase, to point out every weakness in the logic of the proposal. This openness to critique and conflict has made his firm highly successful, even 'fruitful'.

My fear of conflict – my desire for 'blue sky' thinking and 'green light' decisions rather than 'red team' challenge, renders me weaker rather than stronger, and renders my team fragile. You need counsel that will bring conflict. They will challenge you, they will question you, they will bring different perspectives, but they will support you and the calling God has put on your life.

Blue sky Green light Red team

Allow me to get personal and tell you about a member of my inner team. She is one of my most loyal supporters and valuable team members. She carries conflict and counsel in the right balance. She may not know it but she has been one of the main reasons for the growth of vision and culture in the church I lead. I'm pretty sure that when I first arrived in Edinburgh she was not sure – not sure about me and not sure about where we were going – and I knew it. To be honest, I don't blame her. We had what I think was one of the most important meetings of my Edinburgh leadership. Rather than hold her at arm's length out of insecurity, I invited her 'in' to help me lead, to bring her counsel, to support and hone my vision and to voice conflict. I don't want to pretend that it has always been easy, my insecure heart is often tempted to defensive posture and yearns for the superficial peace of 'yes' people. But at its heart, it works brilliantly, it averts strategic disaster and softens the tone of right decisions.

I'm certain that I still struggle with conflict and there are many days when I would rather have an echo chamber, but in an environment of counsel, conflict and critique, we grow – we all grow.

Jesus-leaders look for counsel and encourage conflict and it grows them. It will grow your antifragility.

Who are your counsellors?

How are you dealing with conflict?
Where are you making space for critique?

THE JOY DIMENSION

Jesus not only promises trouble and overcoming. He prophecies joy.

Really? Joy?

Maybe the disciples are reminded of the time Jesus sent the disciples out as 'lambs among wolves' and came home rejoicing (Luke 10:3, 17).

Jesus knows that trials and joy are not mutually exclusive experiences – he also knows that trials without joy will kill you. Testing without joy will result in quitting rather than learning.

We would do really well to disavow ourselves of the common belief in churches that serious purpose is the opposite of serious play. The consequence of this dangerous dualism is that a minority of those I lead carry terminal cases of seriousitus – it's a painful and difficult path in life. Everything is grave and grey when you have seriousitus – your judgment may be keener but your life is more uptight.

Purposeful activity occurs best and is most sustainable in a culture of fun and life; and indeed a life of fun and play with no purpose very quickly becomes no fun at all. Practising the serious discipline of joy will keep you leading when leading sucks. Will keep you learning when learning is hard.

If you or the team you lead has no sense of serious joy, then you need to listen well. This is really important. You will have joy, says Jesus.

Let me illustrate what I mean. Niki and I have spent some time in India over numerous trips. It is here amongst the Jesus-believing Dalit community in the Good Shepherd Churches that I have seen serious joy and serious team spirit. I was speaking at a church gathering in Bangalore. The worship team consisted of street cleaners, sewage workers, young people with no jobs and the staff of Operation Mobilisation. Three things united this group, they were all in the same predicament: they were all poor in the eyes of this world, some living off less than a hundred rupees a day; most lived *en masse* in houses the size of one of our western rooms; and all loved Jesus, following him on his mission.

They started to worship, and it was awful, by any measure of awful. Out of tune and no tune, they strung together ten or so 1980s charismatic choruses.

> One note.
> One beat.
> 30 minutes.

They had no discernable rhythm, they bellowed their praise and danced in their bare feet with joy to the glory of God and then they went out to share Jesus with anyone who would listen, to pray for anyone who wanted and to demonstrate the alive presence of God. They are growing, and learning and planting new churches and discipling new Christians at a rate I can only envy.

The discipline of serious joy

How do you do joy in *Thlipsis*? I'm aware that this could sound flippant, but here goes:

Lighten up

You must create a culture where you don't take yourself too seriously. Where you expose your foolishness and you laugh with others at you. Don't over-spiritualise things or compartmentalise your life. Your job as a leader is not just about getting the job done. When the 'ice bucket challenge' was a thing, we went up on the roof of Central and fifteen of my team soaked me with buckets of ice water while others filmed it. It was well worth an hour of our time and will probably make more impact in eternity than any two-hour staff meeting.

Celebrate

Remember birthdays and celebrate big. The bigger the birthday the bigger the celebration!

Relate

Make it culturally unacceptable to eat lunch at your desk while 'cracking on'. Eat together and talk about what's on TV and who's doing what this weekend. Create a regular social calendar for your team, make it easy. Christmas meals, summer barbeques, Easter picnics.

I have discovered that relational intentionality builds team productivity and enables us to stand in the trial and grow. See when we read the New Testament we are reading the edited highlights of a three-year road trip with Jesus and his team. We are seeing leadership boot camp. I often wonder how much banter, how many campfires, practical jokes and celebrations are assumed but not mentioned?

I am a follower of Jesus and a husband and father before I am leader of the team I have been given. Teams that eat together, celebrate together, that are interested in each other's love lives and marriages and kids and holidays, get the job done better. It's just true. Ask Google or Apple or any company that's beating the system – they treat people like people and not commodities to be traded and used.

THE SECRET IS TRUTH

Jesus seems to suggest here that there is a secret to joy in trials and growing through '*thlipsis*' and becoming antifragile. That secret is truth. Jesus seems to suggest that the right perspective in all of this is a truth that comes through his gift, Holy Spirit.

Holy Spirit is going to help you grow by guiding you into all truth. Look at verse 13: you will know truth, understand truth and speak truth. No hidden stuff, no half-truth. Holy Spirit will clearly expose lies and manipulation and will be so counter-cultural – and that will get you into trouble, which will presumably grow you.

Knowing and doing

But how does truth grow you? I guess it doesn't, in and of itself. Truth only grows you as a leader as you hear it and apply it to your life, acting on it. Growth comes as the fruit of obedience. Knowledge of truth doesn't change us – acting on truth will. As leaders we probably know enough truth to be dangerous, but the reality is that most of us are educated way beyond the level of our obedience. Jesus has already taught his disciples that if they love him they will obey him (John 14:15, 23). Love and obedience cannot be separated.

The greater journey in our leadership lives is not the journey from ignorance to knowledge, but rather from revelation to application. The walk of obedience will grow you in Jesus-leadership. Our modern western cultures tend to recognise a difference between knowing and doing, understanding and acting on the truth of that understanding, yet Jesus is teaching into a culture in which knowledge was never divorced from practice.

If you don't do, you obviously don't know.

Leader, if the Spirit is to be the guide into truth then we must train our hearts and lives for radical obedience or we evidence that we don't really know the Holy Spirit, or, for that matter, truth. Truth will only grow you in the experience of your life. Truth will grow you if it has marinated your life, has been wrestled with, and has proven itself to be dependably authoritative. Don't settle for anything less.

> Don't settle for a lesser kind of simple – that is the enemy of truth.
> Don't settle for a lesser kind of peace – that is the enemy of truth.
> Don't settle for a lesser kind of order – that is the enemy of truth.

Oliver Wendell Holmes, Chief Justice of the Supreme Court of the United States of America, once made a distinction between two kinds of simplicity. He called them 'near side' and 'far side' simplicity.[16] His distinction was between the simplicity of lazy thinking, which relied on shallow-mindedness and purely received understanding; and far side simplicity, that had passed through the crucible of thought and experience and had been proven. Many leaders settle for truth that convinces very few: 'It is because it is because it is'; many others live in complex truth which confuses most and has not been wrestled to the ground in a way that can be lived out. Jesus calls us to a simplicity on the far side of complexity. A simple faith that walks amongst the real fears and doubts of people and speaks profound truth in a way that nurtures understanding. A leadership that is not afraid of questions and conflict, indeed it welcomes debate and doubt. Growth happens best in a culture of questioning – not so much leadership conferences, where the great and the good gather to listen to the better and the best communicate their newest idea – but in environments that promote great questioning and have direct application to your leadership journey.

Learning communities

As a church we have had the privilege of participating in a number of learning communities. These are gatherings of a number of like-minded church leadership teams over a two-year period, gatherings designed to provoke and encourage dreams and plans within a context which allows us to hold each other accountable. The environment created offers an opportunity for a team to gather around some provoking questions that need to be applied to their specific context. Questions like:

- *What if…?* – A challenge to face the brutal facts.
- *What could be?* – An opportunity to dream big.

---

[16] As quoted in John Paul Lederach, *The Moral Imagination: The art and soul of building peace* (OUP, 2005).

- *What will be?* – A space to plan and to be accountable for specific goals.

Leader, if you would grow, you must put yourself in environments where the truth is spoken, wrestled with and applied and where your thinking is stretched. Find them.

This movement towards truth is a hard road because it goes through a road block called control. We are all control freaks – to a greater or lesser extent we all want to control some part of the direction or pace or outcomes of our leadership. It's understandable, and yet if we are unwilling to submit to God's control, timing, or outcomes, we will never fully participate with what he is doing in this world. Control tends to limit conflict; conflict has the potential to sharpen me. Control tends to limit questions which have the potential to develop me. Control tends to want to limit mess which makes space for creativity. I am tempted to desire a lesser simple, a lesser peace, and a lesser order, but the Jesus-leader wrestles for far side simplicity, supernatural peace, and God's order.

Obedience

Train your heart for obedience, to crave truth. Leader, train your heart for obedience. I am a leader of a church because God asked me to be, I stay leading because he hasn't told me I can stop. I lead a church in Edinburgh because he got me by the scruff of the neck and called me there. I don't leave because he hasn't given me permission to do so. Bottom line! I love it as well, but the bottom line is obedience.

I was at a leadership retreat in South Carolina, with a number of senior leaders of large churches. We were sitting by a fire pit talking about what was going on in our churches. I knew that one of the guys led quite a large church, but I didn't know much about him. And as we were spending time, the Holy Spirit said to me, 'Ask him to help you become a better preacher.' I wasn't impressed with the Holy Spirit's idea and I argued with the Holy Spirit and asserted that I was a pretty good preacher, I was not sure I needed help from an American. At which point God insisted. So I went over and spoke to him, and he said he would happily help me and he would listen to my latest talk, so I sent him not my latest talk, but one that I thought was fairly awesome. He listened to it quickly and critiqued it quite firmly and told me that I'd failed his three top tests. I'd failed the beer test, I'd failed the assumptions test and I'd failed the stand-up test.

- The beer test was that within the first minute or so of any talk, he'd worked out whether he wanted to have a beer with the speaker, and he didn't want to have a beer with me because I bored him.
- The second test was the assumptions test, and his statement was that you get what you preach for. I had assumed that everyone in the congregation knew who Jeremiah was, and I was only ever going to get 2% of the nation into any of my gatherings because I wasn't preaching for the 98%.
- And thirdly, I failed the stand-up test. Any non-Christian in America only goes to hear a speaker when that speaker is either a stand-up comedian or an inspirational speaker. And those guys are always exaggerations of their own personalities when they speak. Brian had been with me for a week and recognised that I was a larger than life character, but said that when I get into the pulpit I become less of who I am and not more of who I am. And he said that I failed the test.

So I sulked for a few days before responding to him around his critique. Eventually the Holy Spirit nudged me again and I responded, thanked him, and he said, 'Ok, well just do better next week and I'll listen again.'

So I attempted to do better and he listened again following on from that and he emailed me back and said that it was brilliant and I'd improved in every area and actually the first time he heard me I was really good anyway, he just wanted to find out if I was teachable. And then he invited me to preach in his church in Cincinnati. From that decision to obey the promptings of God, step into risk and swallow my pride, I now have a relationship with both him and with his church, which has changed me and my environment.

Train your heart for obedience. What is God saying? What am I going to do about it? At the core of your leadership practice should always be certain things that you just don't want to do, at times that are not convenient for you to do them, not so that we create a culture of cruelty but we develop muscles of obedience.

Serving someone else's leadership when you have a different, perhaps bigger dream, will train your heart. Learning how to obey the radical inner promptings of the Dove of Truth when it is highly inconvenient and totally embarrassing will train your heart.

Get in shape.

The Holy Spirit is going to speak, but we need to learn to hear what he is saying, and to act appropriately.

You will know that he has become the authority of your life when what he says clashes with the other old authorities – what culture thinks, what tradition says, what your reason makes of it, or what your feelings tell you, or even what your experience up to this point is – and you refuse to lower your understanding of the Word and Spirit to your current thinking or feelings. Will you choose to obey God?

When you have learned to do so as a normal part of your leadership life, you have Holy Spirit muscle memory and you will be living in truth.

What is God saying? What are you going to do about it?

Let me close this chapter by introducing you to a tool for 'Every day is a school day.' Mike Breen and the guys at 3DM teach the principle that God is always wanting to grow us from

Mark 1:15: '"The time has come," he said. "The kingdom of God has come near. Repent and believe the good news!"'

The word 'time' is not the usual Greek word, *chronos*, which refers to the passing of time, but rather the word *kairos*, which is better understood as 'a moment in time,' perhaps a moment when it feels that time stands still, a potential growth moment.

If we recognise and are willing to engage with the growth moment, we can enter a circle of learning. This of course is a choice, every moment is a choice – so often we flatline through our lives rather than engage. If we choose to grow, we enter a learning environment where we first repent: the Greek word *metanoia* means to change the way we think. The Jesus-leader must understand that repentance is a call to constantly change the way we take in reality, that God is speaking constantly, the one who never changes is new every morning. And then we believe, from *pisteo,* meaning to act on that changed thinking, to act in faith. Changing your mind involves observing what God is really saying, reflecting on what that means for us and checking that out with people we trust to make sure we have got this right. Acting in faith on that thought involves planning so that what results is not just an ineffective knee jerk reaction, but accounting for the action so that we really follow through.

Remember, talking about it is talking about it but doing it is doing it!

If every day is really a school day for you as a leader, then the pattern of this model will be repeated in your life daily, as you engage with the trials and the triumphs and the truths of this world and you become more like Jesus.

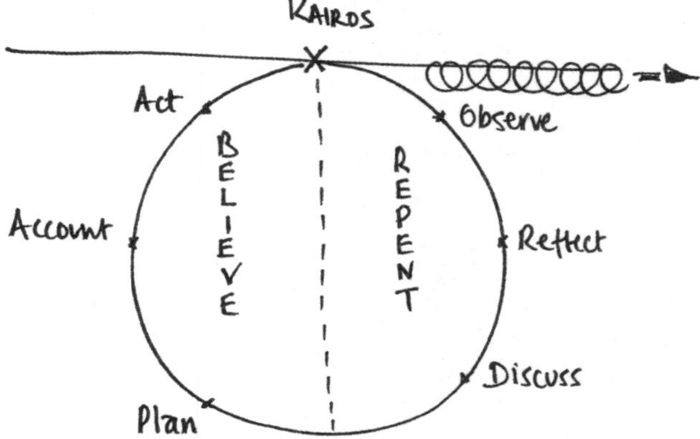

What is God saying?
HEAR

- What do I see?
- What does Scripture say?
- What counsel am I receiving?

What am I doing about it?
OBEY

- How do I need to respond?
- Who will help me follow through?
- What will my breakthrough and faithfulness look like?

'I have given them the glory that you gave me, that they may be one as we are one – I in them and you in me – so that they may be brought to complete unity.'

John 17

5.

SYNCHRONISE

If we all get angry together something might be done.

JRR Tolkien, *The Return of the King*

•

Coming together is a beginning. Keeping together is progress. Working together is success.

Henry Ford

•

'My prayer is not for them alone. I pray also for those who will believe in me through their message, that all of them may be one, Father, just as you are in me and I am in you. May they also be in us so that the world may believe that you have sent me. I have given them the glory that you gave me, that they may be one as we are one – I in them and you in me – so that they may be brought to complete unity. Then the world will know that you sent me and have loved them even as you have loved me.'

John 17:20–23

At the height of a balmy London summer, on 4 August 2012, in the cauldron of sporting brilliance that was the London Summer Olympics, there was a moment of beauty and power that, for me, transcended it all. On the lake at Eton Dorney, Andy Triggs Hodge, Pete Reed, Tom James and Alex Gregory won a rowing gold in the lightweight coxless four. It was all over in 6 minutes 3.97 seconds but those six minutes represented over four years of pain and sacrifice and choices.

It was a beautiful, beautiful moment. I always get emotional on sporting occasions, so I was getting involved, I was standing, I guess with millions, shouting and cheering and crying. And when the camera panned in, there was the kind of pain on their faces that you reserve for some really bad medical condition – the kind of grimace of men who were totally spent, who had given absolutely everything, and every sinew of their bodies had been involved in getting this boat across the line.

But then you looked at the water and it was perfectly still. Rippleless. Because they had learned to row in rhythm.

There is something about working together that changes everything. Were there guys who were rowing in the Olympics who were stronger? Almost certainly. Were there guys who were bigger? I'm absolutely sure there were guys who were bigger. But there was something that had happened in four years of being together, of synchronicity, of aligning themselves, of team, of together – there is something about *together* that changes everything.

Where there is devotion to one another, where there is unity of vision and clarity of individual purpose, with each playing their part, you have something that is bigger than the sum of those parts: you have team.

GLORY

At its best, team is a powerful and beautiful thing. Jesus shows that it can be a glorious thing.

Read John 17 with me.

No, wait.

Before you do, remember that you are on holy ground. Don't just run into this. This is very special. If all Scripture is God-breathed and the encounters in the upper room are God's deep breath, this portion could just be the moment when heaven holds its breath and earth joins in.

This is holy ground. Jesus is praying to the Father, and it is as if we get to listen in.

First, Jesus prays for himself, and he talks to his Father about glory:

> *'Glorify your Son, that your Son may glorify you … glorify me in your presence with the glory that I had with you before the world began …'*
>
> John 17:1, 5

Jesus prays, 'give me glory'.

This is huge, in and of itself. The disciples had heard of glory, all their lives. Glory was something to be marveled at and feared. Glory was the stuff of the temple, the stuff of the holy of holies. Glory was the heart of the most magnificent and odd and incredible stories of Israel's back catalogue. Glory was the stuff of pillars of smoke and fire, of burning bushes and plagues of gnats.

This glory is something God shares with no one (see Isaiah 42:8; 48:11). And yet, Jesus seems to be asking for glory for himself. Jesus is suggesting that he is … God.

The word 'glory' is a translation of the word *doxa,* and forms a massive theme of Scripture, spoken of 275 times in our English Bible. Its meaning is a kind of amalgam of splendour, beauty, radiance, weightiness, purity, worthiness, superiority, majesty. This is not the hollow glory of the rich and famous. It's not celebrity magazine glory. It's not the shallow self-vaunting of fallen humanity. Glory does not equal celebrity. It's God's glory, it's the brightness of his beauty and majesty. It is the wonder of his humanity and it's the mystery of his sacrifice – it is the awe of his grace.

Jesus says glory is to complete the task the Father has given (v. 4). The goal of glory is the finishing of the mission. The job Jesus came to do, the restoration of all things.

The disciples understood something of this. They had been there for much of the build-up. From the call onwards, through Cana (now that's what I call a wedding feast) and Nazareth and the scroll of the prophet Isaiah. And they had joined the dots and done the maths. They had seen blind men see and lame people walk and religious people baulk and a dead man alive again, and it blew up their world.

The hint of everything lost in the Garden of Eden being regained, and the promise of better, the hope of restoration. This is huge. Jesus didn't come to destroy the law or invalidate the prophets. He is the fulfilment. The fulfilment of all the stories and all the traditions and all the religious rituals and symbolism.

This is glory. This is *doxa*.

Glory carriers

And then Jesus goes on to pray for the disciples – and as he prays for their protection and holiness and unity, they might have had an inkling that *they* might be the ones that Jesus is talking to Dad about. And they listen some more, and as they listen, their hearts are encouraged and start to beat faster. Because he's describing them.

And Jesus talks about glory again – glory that has come to him though the disciples, as they believed and accepted and obeyed. What Jesus is saying is that this *doxa* – this glory – is revealed not just through him, in him, but also through the disciples, in his disciples.

And, incredibly, through us. Through your leadership, he is glorified. As we receive and keep his word. At least that's the prayer, that's the plan.

Glory.

We are the glory. And we are to carry glory. Because Jesus then prays for all believers – for us – and says, 'I have given them the glory that you gave me, that they may be one as we are one'.[17] The very same glory you gave me. And that's crazy. Glory. Jesus is saying, 'I'm giving, I'm sharing my glory.' Something incredible is happening.

Stop just a moment.

This glory, that cannot be shared, is being liberally given and preciously entrusted to us. My glory, says Jesus, will be displayed by you. It will be shaped by you. Glory carriers.

He's describing you.

He's revealing his hope and his prayer for your life, for your leadership.

Glory.

As team, in unity, together. Sychronised glory.

Or no glory at all.

THAT THEY MAY BE ONE

The way we build team, work as team, dictates how well we carry glory. You can't fully bear his image or carry his glory alone. God is community and is jealous for the unity of the Church.

It grieves God's heart when we are divided or exclusive; when we describe ourselves in relation to other followers of Jesus by 'what we are not'. When we are judgmental, when we act as snobs, when we duplicate and compete, we are not being Biblical community.

There are more than 41,000 different Christian denominations in the world today.[18] In 1900 there were 1,600, so that's a 2,462% increase in the division of the church over 100 years.

---

[17] John 17:22.

[18] http://christianity.about.com/od/denominations/p/christiantoday.htm

As I stand on the top of Arthur's Seat overlooking the ancient city of Edinburgh, dominant on the skyline are steeples, hundreds of them, beautiful in architectural terms but perhaps not so much in ecclesiastical terms. Because, although Father God has and is redeeming many of the conflicts, almost all of those spires are symbolic of schism and infighting and competition and pride. Many now are luxury flats, high-end restaurants, community theatres, carpet warehouses, indoor climbing centres or even mosques. Jesus wants his bride back and unity and cooperation are at the heart of what it means to be the bride of Christ. It starts with leadership and the heart of leaders.

Your heart.

Competition is anti-kingdom

I know, of course, that there is such a thing as healthy competition – I grew up the oldest of four brothers in a sport-mad family. The stories of my cricketing youth, making my brothers bowl at me for hours and scoring a 'world record' in the garden are legendary in Martin family circles. But competition between brothers and sisters who are essentially after the same goals can become very ugly, very quickly. What is passed off as family competition quickly becomes not only duplication of services and resources, but jealousy and opposition. Unless we are very careful with this, we don't just end up opposing each other and wasting precious kingdom resources in the process, but far more seriously, opposing God.

Competition is anti-kingdom wherever it destroys unity.

How do you know when your competitive spirit is unhelpful? Let me give you some thoughts drawn from my own shameful experience. Have you known what it is like to want another leader to fail, even found yourself not upset by their fall? Have you known what it is like to secretly hope that their latest plant or satellite doesn't quite work out the way they hope? Have you known jealousy over someone else's invitation to speak or have you joined in when the piranhas have devoured an emerging leader over some petty theological slip? I have. It is an ugly, ugly thing and it has no place in Jesus-leadership. Judgment never leads to joy, and jealousy never gives life.

Competition is anti-kingdom because:

- *Jesus is the standard*, and nobody else. Others' success or blessing is really not the benchmark – Jesus is. A huge amount of energy is spent and resources wasted as a result of envy. But Jesus is the benchmark, fix your eyes on him, compare yourself to him. The writer to the Hebrews reminds us to 'run with perseverance the race marked out for us' (Hebrews 12:1). You don't get to run somebody else's race. Envy Jesus, nobody else.
- *I am The Project* – what God is doing with someone else, how he is blessing them or disciplining them is, in essence, none of my business. What God is doing in me and how God wants to refine me and sanctify me *is* my business. I am The Project! Take your eyes off them and fix your eyes on him. 'Each one should test their own actions. Then they can take pride in themselves alone, without comparing themselves to someone else, for each one should carry their own load' (Galatians 6:4–5). This is massive – get it pinned up on your makeup mirror and your shaving mirror, get it in your head and your heart.
- *The body is my body* – what God is doing with someone else is in one sense all of my business. When another person is exalted so am I; when another ministry is successful, so am I. When another brother or sister rejoices or mourns, so do I. We are blood. It's my team.

Unity is massive. There is one thing better than 'embracing the kingdom', and that is 'embracing the kingdom *together*'. The kingdom of God comes when brothers and sisters, in unity, embrace it.

- *Unity is honour* – it is believing the best and speaking the best over everything that God is inspiring and everything God's people are doing.

- *Unity is cheer section* – it is becoming the most obvious vocal supporters of everything that is good and of God in your locality.
- *Unity is compromise and compliment* – it means not needing to have it your way and not needing to have your version of some project or gathering that another part of the body has already set up.
- *Unity is courageous and inspires courage.* Unity makes me brave. Every year, the most courage-inspiring times I experience are gatherings, some local, some national, where I have the privilege of meeting with other leaders. Leaders of different backgrounds, contexts, perspectives and experience, but leaders with a united vison. I have been in a room with Catholic priests, Anglican archbishops, Pentecostal mega-church pastors and emergent planters and I have felt the tangible sense of the Glory of God, and a violent propulsion of the gentle spirit of God into the adventure of God. Unity makes me brave.
- *Unity is visual and vocal and vital.* There is one church in the city – just different expressions. There is one citizenship in heaven – just different testimonies by which we overcame.

TEAM FIRST

In whatever arena you lead, put your team first. Jesus did. He prayed for his team before he prayed for us. He had favourites, or at least that's what it looks like. He loved the crowds, but he appointed seventy-two to go out ahead of him (Luke 10:1), he chose twelve apostles (Luke 6:13) and he spent as much time as possible with three – these were his teams. You can be certain this was not always a popular strategy, I guess there were guys in the seventy-two who wanted to be in the twelve and guys in the twelve who were a bit jealous of the three. Who knows, maybe James wished he was Peter? But Jesus knew that the way to bless the crowds and lead the seventy-two was to prioritise the team.

One of the most inspirational, entrepreneurial leaders in Scotland owns the fastest-growing car dealership business in the country. He is a Jesus-leader and he gets this principle. In the business of selling cars, it's well understood that the customer is king. But in this company, for them, the team is king. Not because he wants to give his customers anything other than a royal experience, but because he knows that he will not be able to do so on a consistent basis, with scalable possibilities, unless his team is king. So he focuses on providing a kingdom class working environment and a great team experience. It is no surprise to me that this Jesus-leader is building a highly successful and talked-about business because he leads like Jesus.

If you prioritise team and do it well, you will enable their leadership, and they will prioritise their teams, who will enable their leadership, and it will touch many. Do this and everyone wins.

HOW DO YOU PICK YOUR TEAM?

Attitude

Jesus had chosen his team way back. We read about the way he did it in Luke 6:12–16. It is interesting to me that he looked around those who were 'disciples' and chose some to be 'apostles'. Disciples were those who had already committed to being under his authority as learners but apostles would be under his authority as they took more authority.

Make sure as you choose a team that you are working with people who have placed themselves under authority before you give them authority.

Character

Mutual submission is such a fundamental tenet of kingdom life that you must not allow anyone to take a position of authority in your team or organisation until you have evidence that they are willing to submit. When the Apostle Paul wants to teach about marriage, he frames the whole of his discourse with the phrase, 'Submit to one another out of reverence to Christ' (Ephesians 5:2). I have suffered repeatedly in my leadership from the vain belief that a leader who would not come under authority could somehow be included in the team in a helpful way and that 'pack therapy' would work it all out. What I have discovered is that an unwillingness to submit to godly leadership is a cancer that destroys leaders and, if unchecked, spreads.

The word 'character' comes originally from the Greek '*kharakter*' which means a stamping tool. It describes an etching of the soul, something that is deeply embedded.

Character ———→ An etching of the soul

Never gamble with character. I have done it a number of times. It hasn't worked.

You need to be able to distinguish between a character fault and a behaviour problem. This is really important. We have all behaved badly and most of us still do. We all do occasional things that are wrong but continuing behavioural issues signal a character fault, that needs to be dealt with, addressed or mended *before* you invite someone on team.

Five 'C's

When choosing people to serve alongside me I have found Bill Hybels' 3 'C's, really helpful:

- *Character* – do I trust them? If I were to put this person under real pressure what do I think will come out?
- *Competence* – can they do the job? If I appoint them, will that department or ministry take off?
- *Chemistry* – will we gel? If we include this person will they increase or decrease the sense of family?

To these three Cs, I would like to offer an extension.

- *Capacity* – what can they carry? Can this person keep pace with the team and carry their weight or will we have to make allowances? In the teams I lead, everyone has to pull their weight, everyone must carry. No prima donnas allowed. There are some jobs that no one wants to do and everyone must do: stacking chairs, welcoming people, serving food and cleaning up are 'All Play' events for the team.
- *Catalyzing* – how will they add? What will this person bring that is not already in the team, and how will that release other gifts?

- Character
- Competence
- Chemistry
- Capacity
- Catalyzing

Leader, pick your team well because they will become your family.

Inheriting a team

What if you can't choose your own team? I'm sure some of you reading this, like me, inherited a team, a team you might not have chosen. The only difference inheriting a team makes is time. As the leader you are still responsible for getting the right team and finding their right fit and dealing with character and behaviour issues. They need to become your team.

I am of course aware that some of you are reading this and thinking 'But I don't have people around me – it's OK for the leader in a large organisation with a big team'. Yet Jesus looked around his environment and called what appears to be a random, disheveled and unqualified crew to be his team. There are always people around willing to be involved in a God-given venture if you look hard enough, submit wide enough and die well enough. You may not be able to pay them, they may not always want to run with your scheme, they may take careful management and strong leadership, but where God births a vision and raises a leader, he always provides a team. They may be in your biological family; they may not yet even know Jesus.

Find them. Submit to them.

The law of the space

When it comes to teams, choosing the right people is possibly the most important decision you will make. Leaving a space for the unlikely leader is just as crucial. Flying in the face of popular cultural wisdom, Jesus-leaders look beyond the obvious successes to back the potential in the unlikely choice.

Jesus chose a couple of fisherman brothers at the core, and collaborators, cheats, terrorists and skeptics as the outriders, all with limited training or experience to bring, to lead the most important family ever and help him save the world. Jesus seems to work with whoever he has within his reach. You don't need a nationwide search for the best of the best or a huge recruitment budget.

You need faith and a space.

Make a space, just one, in your leadership team for the one you are not sure of. Make sure character is certain and take a punt on potential. One of my strongest and most reliable team members came into the team by the law of the space. He didn't know it at the time but now he would be one of the first I lean on and the one I trust to carry.

FIT TEAMS

The best teams are holy teams.

Jesus prays for sanctification for his team (John 17:17). You are the glory, and you are to display glory. He loves you too much to allow you to be less than who you are.

The word 'holy' is the word *hagiouzo.* It means to sanctify and consecrate, to separate or set apart for a particular purpose. What Jesus is wanting to do with you and your team is to make you fit for purpose. He is wanting to root out anything that is incompatible with him and get you spiritually ripped so you can cooperate with him in the glory thing.

The best teams are fit teams. Fit for purpose in every way.

These teams see holiness as being as much about physical fitness and radical generosity and community fun, as it is about behaving right – maybe even more so! Jesus is really interested in your team being fit for purpose.

The best teams are fit teams.

Emotionally fit

One of the key verses in the Scriptures for leadership is Proverbs 4:23.

'above all else guard your heart for it is the well spring of life' proverbs 4:23

Your heart, how you feel, directs your paths. Everything else flows from this place. You need a healthy heart if you are going to encourage healthy team, if you are to have healthy leadership. I'm not sure how much we really value this in our culture. We guard almost everything else at great cost: we guard property with alarm systems and padlocks and insurance; we guard health with vitamins and minerals, but we leave our hearts untended.

It is as much value to your team to provide time and space to listen to people's hearts and be concerned for the emotional health of those you lead as it is to pay them right or train them up. One of the most useful habits of my week is simply to walk around the offices at Central and observe and listen. In turn I am expecting my team leaders to be the custodians of their team's emotional fitness.

How do you guard your heart?

Physically fit

Fit body, fit mind! Create a culture where fitness goals and challenges are a highly acceptable part of the team's life. We encourage charity runs and walks and the training that comes with it. Do all you can to create a culture of physical health in your team. The encouragement of exercise and the discouragement of unhealthy eating is an environment that is set up to promote health in every other arena of life.

I know that if I am not eating well and exercising well then I am not functioning well anywhere else. Have you noticed how many of the activities of the church and particularly of leadership in the church involves cake or cookies? One of the early attempts at a physically fit staff team at Central was to replace the cake with fruit and start having meetings where we didn't have to eat and drink.

One of my closest friends owns a business where they take this so seriously that they now offer to pay part of a critical illness and life assurance cover policy that has lifestyle and fitness benefits built in. The policy gives you an incentive to lose weight, exercise and quit smoking. The result is a fitter, happier and more productive team.

Financially fit

Fit finances mean fit lives. Create a culture where it is more than acceptable to encourage stewardship and generosity, and where financial conversations are not off the table. Bad financial decisions can cripple people and will have an adverse effect on your team. Be aware that if you pay your staff badly, you dishonour them, you make it difficult for them to do anything other than struggle, and, ultimately, you ensure that they will not do a good job for you.

The fitness conversation

The place we set up to have these conversations is something we call 'huddle', a vehicle where we seek to keep the team accountable for development in character and skills. We meet regularly to ask those questions. 'What is God saying and what are you doing about it?' And nothing is off the table. Every leader in our church family is in a huddle which meets regularly to encourage fitness.

SECURE TEAMS

As you lead your team, they must increasingly know how appreciated they are. How much they belong. Teams that really are family will tend to be loyal and fruitful. But teams where there is insecurity about identity or role will end up destroying each other.

I have discerned, through numerous mistakes, a number of keys to security in my team.

Communication

Great communication is an absolute necessity for great leadership. What is also true is that you will never get it quite right. Communication will always be the stick that some – often those who don't like the change you are bringing or the way you are leading – will beat you with. If your team is to feel secure and therefore trust you to lead them, they must be in the know. They must feel honoured and trusted with knowledge that brings freedom, trusted to choose to follow rather than being kept in the dark and treated as minions.

over communicate
over communicate
over communicate

I produce a weekly video to all leaders in our church to go alongside the regular e-bulletin. My ambition is to communicate what is on my heart, but above all to say again and again how much I appreciate who the team is, what the team stands for and what the team does. What you say and how you say it matters, more than you know. Vocabulary creates culture – it always does.

Clear and concise communication is absolutely vital if you are to create a culture of security. If people know what is expected, to what quality and by when, and what the consequences of missing the deadline are, then they will perform.

Championing

Defend your team. Sort out weaknesses in private so you can always speak positively in public.

Your team need to know that you are for them, want the best for them and that you have their back. Speak well of your team – as Americans are fond of saying, 'brag on' your team. Speak well of them when they are present so they can hear what you think. It is incredible how much taller team members walk when they know they are valued and loved.

Give courage to your team by encouraging them. I would like to redeem the word encourage – it is over-used and often misunderstood to mean 'say nicey-nicey things and be pleasant in the family of God's people.' But truly encouraging words, words that breed courage, are like breathing gasoline onto a flickering flame. They cause tea-lights to become flame throwers. If you love your team, tell them. If they do a good job, praise them.

Be specific with your encouragement, be laser-like. Depending upon which gurus you read and which ones you believe, it seems you need somewhere between forty and fifty positive comments to counter every negative critique. I'm not absolutely sure that that is true – I think it's more. 'Cos my heart, and probably yours, hears and holds the negative in a very different way than it hears and holds the positive. It is almost as if your heart nurtures the negative. Leaders don't have generalised opposition. They have very specific laser-like accusers. Every developing leader in your charge needs to hear and hold laser-like encouragement.

Be specific.

How are they growing?

What examples do you have of success?

When did they bless you and why?
Tell them.

Constancy

When Niki and I moved to Edinburgh we knew that the job that the Lord had called us to was bigger than us and longer than us. This was a thirty-year call or a two-year call, depending on whether or not what God had asked of us was embraced by the people we had been called to lead. It was with real enthusiasm that, at our first annual vision meal and two years into our time, I stood before the church and announced that unless God called us very clearly to another role, Scotland was stuck with us for the rest of our ministry.

Recently I was given a word from an American leader, gifted in prophecy. We were in a seafood restaurant in a marina on the west coast of Scotland. The conversation went something like this:

'*Karl, God can't bless your Plan A whilst you have your Plan B in your back pocket.*'

As I was receiving that word, he decided to tell me what my Plan B was,

'*You are afraid that your audacious vision for the Celtic lands will be rejected and you will have to lead a church in the US who will materially look after your family.*'

It was outrageous. And he was absolutely right. I had never articulated Plan B, not even to myself. But I had it in my back pocket to use. 'In emergency, break glass!'

And he still hadn't finished.

'*God can't ever bless your Plan B, because it's not his plan. When are you going to buy your grave plot in Scotland?*'

Wow…

Lose the back-up plan.

If those you lead think you might leave, they will not follow, not fully, and your Plan A will remain 'unblessed'.

GLORY TEAMS

Jesus is interested in producing teams of glory. All glory flows from one place, from the heart of God, from the relationship and purpose of God.

'... *that they may be one as we are one.*'

verse 11

The secret to joy and sanctification and mission and glory is oneness.

And oneness is all about relationship.

It is all about intimacy. The effectiveness of your team, the effectiveness of leadership, always comes back to intimacy. When we try and do unity outside of intimacy, it kills the life of Christ. We so easily end up with functional teams and lowest common denominator agreements. But if it flows out of oneness, it is a thing of the spirit and produces life and witness.

For your team to be glory carriers – joyful, purposeful, holy, secure glory carriers – you must do serious business with the fact that Jesus 'only does what the Father tells him'. This is huge. How can we, as teams, develop a way of being that enables the Father to speak and his children to listen, respond, obey and act?

The team is responsible for the team as far as the team's walk with Jesus is concerned – this is the number one fitness concern. The fit team has zero tolerance for cynicism about the pursuit of God. This may sound like a surprising statement but in my experience it's not always easy to keep it real when your faith and your job collide.

It took me much longer than I am proud of to discover how important communal habits of prayer and worship and Bible reading are for any team seeking to serve God. My teams now meet at the start of the workday for a thirty-minute devotional time, where we set ourselves apart as individuals and as a team for the cause of Christ. We interrupt our days at midday to say the Lord's prayer and remind ourselves of what we are doing and for whom. We have created a devotional called *Rooted* for the whole church – you can get the app at https://rooted.org.uk. We also email the Bible verses for each day to the whole church and offer regular commentary. We encourage an evening *examen*, 'What has God been saying to me today?' 'What am I going to do about it?'

Leader, have your team hang out with Jesus. Scripture tells us that as we do, we become like him.

How can your team become a 'glory team'?

- Create some regular expressions of corporate worship, prayer, Bible reading and rededication in your rhythms and patterns of life. Find out what works best for your team.
- Find ways to retreat. Retreat alone and retreat as a team. Sometimes you just need space for the Father to speak … and for you all to listen.
- Encourage your team to hang out with Jesus; he is the glory carrier.

Jesus gathered a group of individuals and made a team of world changers. They planted the church. Not *a* church. *The* church. It changed everything. That is always Jesus' strategy. To take some individuals and to inspire them to be team to carry glory and to serve his kingdom. Whether that grouping is a Benedictine order, a Moravian mission team, a Clapham sect, a YWAM team or a Baptist Church plant, it's still the way that Jesus builds his church. Whether that grouping is an executive board, a staff team, a rugby squad or a family unit, it's still the way that Jesus is extending his kingdom. It's still the way that his people are to carry glory.

6.

SKIRMISH

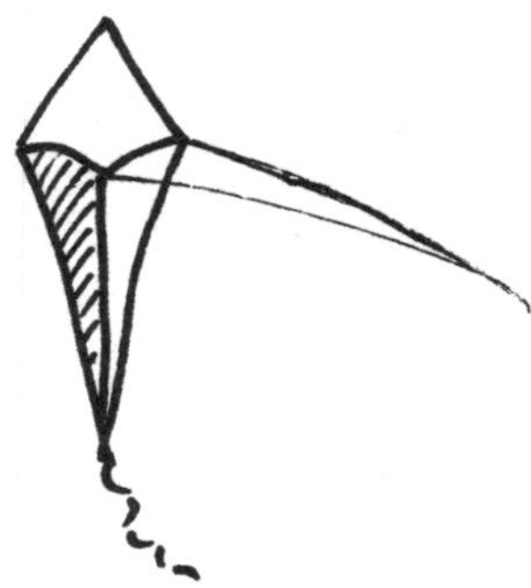

A certain amount of opposition is a great help to a man. Kites rise against, not with, the wind.

Lewis Mumford

•

We are always on the anvil; by trials God is shaping us for higher things.

Henry Ward-Beecher

•

Now Judas who betrayed him, knew the place, because Jesus had often met there with his disciples …

John 18

Now Judas, who betrayed him, knew the place, because Jesus had often met there with his disciples. So Judas came to the garden, guiding a detachment of soldiers and some officials from the chief priests and the Pharisees. They were carrying torches, lanterns and weapons.

Jesus, knowing all that was going to happen to him, went out and asked them, 'Who is it you want?'

'Jesus of Nazareth,' they replied.

'I am he,' Jesus said. (And Judas the traitor was standing there with them.) When Jesus said, 'I am he,' they drew back and fell to the ground.

Again he asked them, 'Who is it you want?'

'Jesus of Nazareth,' they said.

Jesus answered, 'I told you that I am he. If you are looking for me, then let these men go.' This happened so that the words he had spoken would be fulfilled: 'I have not lost one of those you gave me.'

Then Simon Peter, who had a sword, drew it and struck the high priest's servant, cutting off his right ear. (The servant's name was Malchus.)

Jesus commanded Peter, 'Put your sword away! Shall I not drink the cup the Father has given me?'

Then the detachment of soldiers with its commander and the Jewish officials arrested Jesus. They bound him and brought him first to Annas, who was the father-in-law of Caiaphas, the high priest that year. Caiaphas was the one who had advised the Jewish leaders that it would be good if one man died for the people.

Simon Peter and another disciple were following Jesus. Because this disciple was known to the high priest, he went with Jesus into the high priest's courtyard, but Peter had to wait outside at the door. The other disciple, who was known to the high priest, came back, spoke to the servant-girl on duty there and brought Peter in.

'You aren't one of this man's disciples too, are you?' she asked Peter.

He replied, 'I am not.'

It was cold, and the servants and officials stood round a fire they had made to keep warm. Peter also was standing with them, warming himself.

John 18:2–18

Have you ever been in a situation when somebody else got your prophetic word? The word that you thought should come to you? I was travelling with my friend in the United States and we had gone to see a well-known leader who I knew would have input for me. Sure enough, on the final morning we came down to be greeted by, 'I had a dream of the two of you last night'. He turned to my friend and said he saw him as a presidential leader with great wisdom to whom people would come for insight and leadership.

That was *my* word!

I was sure that he'd got the wrong person. To compound the slight, he turned to me, 'and you …' he said, 'are a pirate'. My face must have dropped. 'No, it's a good thing.' He went on, 'Your job is to command an ugly crew and many pirate ships. And take back from the enemy everything that has been stolen from the people of God. You are a pirate.'

Leadership is pirating. You are in a war. This is not a peacetime effort. It is going to get ugly.

'on the night that Jesus was betrayed…'

Almost every week in church we hear the words 'On the night that Jesus was betrayed, he took the bread and, when he had given thanks, he broke it.' These are words that, if you've grown up in church, or if you have hung around church at all, you will have heard hundreds and hundreds, maybe even thousands of times. Paul writes this in 1 Corinthians 11.

But here's the question. Why did Paul choose to use that particular phrase, 'On the night that Jesus was betrayed'? Why did he choose to use that phrase to glorify this supper that we celebrate, this bread and this wine, this community thing? I mean, there were better things that he could have said: 'On the night that Jesus washed his disciples' feet and showed how much he loved them.' Or, 'On the night that Jesus prayed in the garden and prayed to the Father …' or, 'On the night that Jesus was arrested and tried and set out towards the cross, he broke bread.' Any of these other things would have elevated this supper.

But Paul writes, 'On the night Jesus was betrayed …'

Why betrayed?

I think Paul is saying: I want you to remember – for ever – that this community that we are part of, that this community who we identify with, that this community who we lead, is the community of the betrayed one. The one who was let down by those who were closest to him. This is so important.

THE LEADERSHIP OF THE BETRAYED

If you want to bear the light of the world, to lead in such a way that allows him to shine, you are going to have to walk through the darkness. There is no other way. That's what light is for, illuminating darkness. But the darkness can be a pretty lonely place.

As we meet Jesus on this particular night, there is darkness everywhere. Not so much physically, because it was Passover, the time of the full moon. The night was not really dark. Yet there is darkness all over this piece.

Betrayal by one of his own. Abandonment from most of his team. Denial from his closest friend. There is the darkness of manipulation from the leaders of God's people. Large and looming over this narrative are the fingerprints of the enemy of God.

Dark prints.

Satanic forces, institutional powers, spiritual leaders.

And yet Scripture reveals Jesus walking head first into the darkness in order to bring his light. That's what he's doing, he's bringing the light of the world to bear on the darkness of human experience.

And that's what I do … and so do you. As you lead, you are supposed to shine. Wherever it is dark, Jesus-leadership is needed. Light leadership. The leadership of light.

It's dark for kids who are waiting to be fostered and adopted, it takes light-filled Jesus-leaders to shine. For addicts who have limited facilities to get dry and get free – it takes light-filled Jesus-leaders to start detox facilities and ministries. It's dark for people imprisoned in debt – it takes Jesus-filled light-filled leaders who will walk into darkness and shine. It's dark for marriages broken with no one to listen – it takes light-filled marriages to get alongside dark ones for hope to come. It's dark for people who have no one to introduce them to Jesus, because no one in their family has ever heard of him. It's going to take leadership. Light leadership in darkness.

Light in darkness.

Face the brutal facts

You need to know the nature of the opposition you face. For Jesus here in this passage, opposition comes from three directions.

- He is going to face outright attack, full frontal opposition which is designed to take him out.
- He is also going to have to deal with the darkness of betrayal from within his close team.
- He is going to walk with disappointment as he is let down by friends and followers.

Get ready

'When he had finished praying, Jesus left' (John 18:1).

He got ready.
So must you.

He got ready in prayer.
So must you.

You see this is not a battle you can win. It was not a battle Jesus thought he could win, without the Father.

Jesus-leaders win spiritual battles on their knees. It has always been so. The Apostle Peter is angelically released from Herod's prison as the people of God fight darkness on their knees (Acts 12). Every biblical revival and every historical awakening recorded has its birth and sees its victory as Jesus-leaders pray, like Jesus.

Opposition will come, but you can be ready. You don't build a shelter in the storm – you build one before the storm comes. And you *will* experience storms. Jesus had prayed and built his team and worked out his authority long before the clouds gathered. Before the storm came.

Do the same.

- Establish a pattern of prayer now. You won't do it when the storm hits. What does it look like?
- Develop a team of support now. When the storm comes it will be too late to look around. Who are they?
- Secure the authority of your life now. What you will stand on now. When the storm comes, if you find yourself standing on the wrong ground, you will not stand for long. What do you believe about God? Write it down … now.

Survive the storm

I remember with sickness the night I received the phone call and subsequent visit that told me that the man we had befriended and welcomed into our home, and who had become friendly with our young family, was a paedophile who had been abusing children for years and was probably waiting for his opportunity with ours. I still feel sick writing this.

call with pain the times that close friends, having usly supported me, undermined me and my leadership lly. I think of numerous public confrontations and private email exchanges which have hurt and done damage because they came from family – so close. I'm sure that you have many stories of your own.

There are three things that keep me walking in the storm:

- The surety of what I believe about God.
- The fellowship of those I have gathered around me.
- The certainty of the call of God on my life to lead.

Sometimes all you can do is survive in the storm. And if you survive the storm, you can thrive after the storm.

All the best opportunities come later. Later, when you have the scars associated with the storm you will have strength and testimony and wisdom. You will have developed 'standing in the storm' muscles and a 'standing in the storm' story that can be passed on. You will have experience and confidence that can be leveraged.

Sometimes you just need to know how to survive.

DIRECT ATTACK

Judas came to the garden, guiding a detachment of soldiers and some officials from the chief priests and the Pharisees. They were carrying torches, lanterns and weapons.

> *Jesus, knowing all that was going to happen to him, went out and asked them, 'Who is it you want?'*
>
> John 18:4

There is no doubt here who the enemy is and what the enemy wants. The religious leaders had been plotting for some time to overthrow Jesus. He is a threat to their way of being and their livelihood. But now they fully expose themselves. Jesus' light shines even in their darkness.

What can we learn here?

Know who the enemy is

To my shame, I have frequently mistaken my friends for my foes and my foes for my friends. Jesus had taught the disciples that 'whoever is not against you is for you' (Luke 9:50). Equally, and as if to clarify things, Jesus says a short while later to the same guys, 'Whoever is not with me is against me' (Luke 11:23).

In short, work out who your enemy is.

I have spent far too much time in leadership worrying about the soundness or otherwise of other Jesus-leaders and in my heart condemning people as my enemy, when in reality they are my brothers and sisters. I have read too many books, paid attention to too many blogs and heard more talks than I would care to admit, whose sole aim appears to be to demonise other leaders that I will spend eternity with. All the time the real enemy rubs his hands, employs his dark arts and gets about his business, and the dark gets darker and the light is employed in the wrong direction. If indeed it shines at all. Work out who the enemy is and who the allies are. And shine in darkness. What beliefs are worth losing family over?

Write them down.

Fight from a place of victory

Fight from a place of victory rather than towards it. Don't fight to prove anything. Fight to secure something. Jesus had complete confidence in who he was and knew what was going to happen.

The attack from the front is aimed at destroying you. In reality all it can do is distract you. The enemy can't destroy you. Darkness can't destroy light nor can it coexist with light. A significant weapon that the enemy will employ to distract you is to undermine your secure footing. Jesus knows who he is and where he is going (John 13), all that is going to happen to him (John 18), and he knows who the enemy is. He is fighting from the position of a victory already won that needs secured and not from the position of a defeat.

Leader, the war has already been won. It is won on the cross. The battles you fight now are just skirmishes designed to limit your breakthrough and undermine your fruitfulness.

Take your stand on the victory already won and know the enemy. I have an internal battle every week before I preach. The enemy whispers to me, 'Who are you to say this? What you have is pitiful and uninspiring.' So I kneel and I focus. I determine to stand and deliver what Father God has given me. I kneel and then I stand.

And after I preach he comes again and says, 'I told you so'. We play this game every week. He tempts every time. He loses every time. Every time I kneel and focus and stand and serve for an audience of one. He loses. It's a skirmish every week. But the war has already been won. And each time I refuse to give in, I pattern my life towards victory.

BETRAYED FROM WITHIN

You will experience betrayal. Have you ever been betrayed – I mean really stabbed in the back? It's amazing how devastating that can be. Rejection and abandonment, if left to fester, have the potential to wreck teams and callings and the ability to destroy community. The moment that you allow people in, you create the potential for pain and loss as much as joy and gain.

Break bread … together

Jesus knew who would betray him, maybe when he chose him, I guess when he gave him authority, certainly when he washed his feet, and broke bread with him. When Judas kisses him, I wonder whether Proverbs 27:6 came into his mind and stuck in his throat, 'Wounds from a friend can be trusted but an enemy multiplies kisses.'

The wounds that come from friends, family, or those who are supposed to love us, always hurt the most, cut the deepest and leave the most difficult scars. Jesus-leaders are going to be betrayed and hurt and let down.

Fact.

Unfortunately, in our broken world, that is just truth. Trust and loyalty are so huge in the arsenal of team, that when they are abused or absent it can cause far greater impact than the initial betrayal. The challenge for leadership is that unless we manage betrayal well, we can become cynical or hard-hearted and not open to the kind of relationship that brings life to a team. We shut down the potential of great leadership and kingdom breakthrough and we allow a negative moment to have an eternal impact. The danger is that the first time it happens we walk away and as a result become lone wolf leaders. That's not Jesus' way.

Jesus steps down out of heaven, he empties himself, he lives this incredible life, he teaches a people who will not listen, he loves the people who will reject him, he demonstrates the Father to the people who spit on him, revile him, who yell, 'Crucify!' And he eats – he eats, almost the most intimate thing you can do – he eats with these people. He breaks bread and then he breaks himself. He eats with these people and then he dies for these people. These people that he knows will leave him.

Have you ever let him down? I have.

Every time I don't act with compassion, every time I don't operate out of oneness with Jesus, every time I have not lived out of the fullness of Jesus Christ, I let him down. Every time I don't share what I have, I let him down. Every time I don't love other people, every time I judge somebody, I let him down. Every time I have an opinion which I hold too strongly, which hurts somebody, I let him down. Every time I operate out of an orphan spirit and entertain jealousy or competition, and every time I hold on to unforgiveness, every time I view myself differently to the way that Jesus views me, every time I think of myself as stupid or fat or ugly, every time I do that, I let him down. Every time I let anyone else down, I let him down.

Have you ever let anyone else down? Have you ever betrayed them or denied them, or excluded them or abandoned them or neglected them? I have. I've let some of my closest friends down.

Has anyone ever let you down?

Put your sword away

I absolutely love Peter, because Peter is an all-in kind of guy. If Jesus was to say, 'Jump!' Peter would say, 'Off what building do you want me to jump? I don't care what it is, just tell me later on because I'm in. I'm fully in.' And Peter is so all-in, that when he sees Jesus being attacked, Jesus being threatened, he takes a sword out and he is straight in there and he cuts off an ear. I like Peter for that. I know I shouldn't but I like Peter for that. I think, come on! It is better than running away – at least you are doing something. And Jesus says, 'Peter, would you put away your sword. Peter, the kingdom of God is from another world. It just doesn't work like this.'[19]

Have you ever lopped off somebody's ear, in the hope of doing some good for the Saviour of the world? Because I have. Righteously. Given them a talking to. Thought the worst of them, assumed their intentions were bad. It's not the way of the Saviour of the world. We are a community of the betrayed ones. It's almost as if we should wear that as a badge of honour. We are a community of the ones who have been let down and who have let people down and yet who have experienced healing and forgiveness and grace and mercy. And we get to carry forgiveness and grace and mercy.

---

[19] Or something like that – my paraphrase.

Put your sword down.
Put your sword down.

Never defend yourself. Never become defensive. I have learned this the hard way! At the core of his five rules of life, AW Tozer lived by this maxim: 'Never defend yourself'. I try to lead with that rule. My role as a leader is to defend others and to fight for their God-given vision. My calling as leader is to provide and protect DNA and culture which creates the environment in which dreams flourish. If I spend my time defending myself, or the vision God has given, I show that it's my vision and not God's. If he gave it, and he wants it to be, then he can defend it. Don't defend yourself – let God do it – he is more than able.

I have found that becoming defensive cements me into a position from which I find it difficult to move or grow and tends to provoke the mirror reaction in those I perceive to be attacking me. Nobody wins, the vision is not embraced and the strategy is not advanced.

I have discovered that when I refuse to become defensive, the opportunity for movement on both sides, learning, resolution and growth, is greatly enhanced.

'Never defend yourself' does not mean 'Shut up', not always, especially if to be silent means that your non-verbal communication screams!

Find out what your attacker needs from you in order to help them grow.

- They need you to not take it personally when it isn't. More often than not, my experience has been that an attack from someone I have been attempting to lead is not motivated by hatred of me, but fear of change or misunderstanding of my motives. There will be times when the attack is purely malicious. If it is, suck it up, take it on the chin and close the conversation as quickly as possible.

- They need you to admit fault where there is fault. 'Fess up – sometimes that just releases the pressure valve. Never do this as a tactic, though, only do it when it's the truth.
- They need you to clarify your motive – with grace. They need to know why you did what you did and what you meant to achieve, no more, no less. Clarify.
- They need you to bring peace. Jesus-leaders always bring peace – because Jesus is the Prince of Peace. Do all you can to bring and bear peace. Peace is not the absence of conflict but the presence of God in conflict. There will be peace – not an uneasy, superficial peace but a peace through conflict.

So put your sword down.

Watch your mouth

I find, more often than not, my sword is my mouth. My most deadly weapon is my tongue. For me to be a peacemaker often means learning to be silent when I know that I can destroy with words.

I have discovered that this posture helps build strategy rather than wreck projects. Try it.

Stick to the plan

The religious leaders have been trying to set Jesus up for months now, they have been trying to rig stuff and they've been trying to organise stuff and they basically want Jesus dead because he is irritating. They are the religious leaders and they just hate him. But things have happened so quickly[20] that they didn't even have time to get the Sanhedrin together, the seventy-one teachers of the law, the elders and religious scribes that they

---

[20] Some commentators suggest that they had decided not to try to arrest Jesus during the feast, but the opportunity provided by Judas came as a surprise. It was no surprise to Jesus.

needed to get together to organise something so they could condemn Jesus. They didn't have time for that. They didn't have time to inform Pilate properly. And he's the only one who could give the death sentence. They certainly didn't have time to rig the trial effectively, it just kind of happened. It was the ultimate in opportunism for them.

And the disciples – they weren't ready. Jesus has been encouraging them to prepare themselves for his leaving. They should have been ready but they just weren't. It was Passover and it was heaving and a party was going on and it was chaos everywhere.

In the chaos there is a plan. Hatched in the heart of God, hinted at by the prophets, and heard, ironically, on the lips of Jesus' arch accuser, Caiaphas.[21]

'It would be good if one man died for the people.'

Now that's a plan.

A dying and a rescuing, a bridging of an unbridgeable gap, a forgiveness possible because the debt had been paid, victory possible because death had been defeated.

> A plan so simple,
> for you and I to know God,
> to walk with him,
> to have his character grow in us.
> To represent him to the world.

We are the plan and we carry the plan. Leader, you are the plan and you need a plan. Everything in this world will move towards chaos, will morph towards complexity. We are dealing with broken people in a dying world. But you are the plan and your leadership will stand or fall on your ability to clarify the plan and stick to it.

---

[21] John 11:50; 18:14.

You need a plan. It may be as simple as '*X to Y by When*'. But you need a plan. I hear too many people with a vision that is huge and no plan at all. We are going to change the world by this time next year, but we are not quite sure how.

Clarify your measurable win

I once heard an expert in church planting and church growth encourage his listeners to 'Clarify your measurable win.' He emphasised each word in turn: 'clarify', 'measurable' and 'win', asserting that each one was crucial for the forming of a plan that will give feet to your vision.

Clarify your measurable win

What?
Why?
How?
Who?
When?
Where?

What is your win?

What is really important, what really matters in your context, in your leadership? What difference does your team need to make?

Make it clear and simple

Make it repeatable and memorable. So that others might buy in. You don't need your clarity to be complete. You just need it to be clear. Ask yourself some questions: What? Why? How? Who? When? Where?

Make it measurable

How will you know whether you have done this? Remember what you count counts? Of course the difficulty in ministry terms is that many of our goals would have qualitative measurables as much as quantitative measurables. It is easier to count people and money than discipleship. Don't use that as an excuse. If you don't count – you will never know.

Find a way to measure life and growth and depth. And when you find it, share it with other leaders. It will be valuable beyond belief.

You may get a revelation but unless you have a strategy it will become at best redundant and at worst a frustration for you and those you lead.

DISAPPOINTED FROM BEHIND

Losing followers

Some of the greatest challenges of my leadership haven't come front on, or even from those who have betrayed me, but rather from the disappointment and attrition of those who follow.

My record in losing people isn't so good, so I have to be careful here not to be justifying my dysfunctionality. As Central has grown over the years, we have had hundreds of people join and hundreds leave. Honestly, when that happens for the first time, when someone you have loved and tried to lead leaves, it hurts. A lot.

Many have left for good reason – we have propelled hundreds of students into kingdom futures and dozens of apprentices into leadership beyond Edinburgh. But some have just been upset by changes in the way we are church, the volume of the music or an emphasis on a particular value or vision, and they have left. I have had 'Baptists' leave, because my leadership was too directive, I have had 'new church' people leave because I was not strong enough in my directive leadership. I have had 'conservatives' leave because I was far too experiential in my approach to ministry and 'charismatics' leave because all the experience was not for experience's sake but to propel us into the world. I have had 'emergents' come around the church because we were doing interesting cultural things and then leave because we still believed and practised ancient orthodox truth. I will probably have others leave after reading this book.

Not least because I just labelled people!

I try and encourage myself that I am in good company.

People rejected Jesus, so much so that Jesus asked his disciples if they wanted to go too (John 6:67)! Followers also left Paul, to the extent that he felt abandoned towards the end of his ministry (2 Timothy 4:9–11). Unless you feel that you are a better or more trusted leader than Jesus or Paul, you will have to steel yourself for rejection, abandonment and betrayal.

Jesus-leadership will always attract and repel people, often in equal measure, and yet many leaders make it the gold standard of their ministry to have kept everyone together. Jesus does say, 'I have not lost one of those you gave me,'[22] but only after many had left. Could it be that some you are striving to hold on to are not those you have been given? Of course it may also be the case that you kept everyone together and didn't take them anywhere.

---

[22] John 18:9, but see also 17:12.

I have had many letters and emails and public dressings-down in church meetings, reminding me that I was destroying someone's church and asking me who I thought I was to try to lead in such a way. If you are a leader who has tried to bring about change you can probably add your own story here. If you are doing your job well, someone, somewhere is going to leave you.

It may not be fair and it almost certainly isn't justified (although in my case I'm sure it sometimes was) but this is the territory and the stuff of Jesus-leadership. We are the community of the betrayed.

Choose who to lose

You get to choose who you are going to lead and who is going to leave. In truth you have to, or it will happen by default.

Possibly the most helpful advice my father gave me as I started out in ministry was to tell me the story of Napoleon's army. I am not sure to this day whether the story has any semblance of truth to it, but the strategy works. The story goes that Napoleon would divide his army into thirds:

- A third of his forces would attack the enemy – the moment they saw the enemy. There was no holding them back. They were so ready for the fight they were almost uncontrollable.
- A third of his forces would desert the moment they saw the enemy. They were so full of fear or had no real loyalty they would want to run away.
- And a third of his forces would be waiting to see which of the other groups was going to win the argument, and the day, and then just fall in with them.

My father asserted that this was just like leading any church or team. There is a proportion of the team that is so for you and for the vision that they are almost uncontrollable in their enthusiasm. These are followers – future *leaders* – and they need training. There is another section, the *leavers*, who are just fearful and against anything you are saying and doing as a leader and want to run away – or, more specifically, they want you and your dream to leave. Finally, of course there is the majority, the *learners*, that will just follow whichever group is going to be allowed to lead.

He went on to say that most Christian leaders spend most of their time and resources trying to appease the second group, to stop the people who want to leave from leaving. Three things always follow this kind of leadership:

> *The leaders*, who are up for the fight and ready to follow, leave. You did not lead them. They leave because they were not invested in, not permissioned not resourced. They leave to be around a leader who will prioritise time and give vision to release their leadership.
>
> *The learners* are waiting to learn. What they learn is that if you act as if you might leave, if you are cynical about the leader or the vision then you get the time and attention of leadership, so they begin to foster a culture of negativity and complaint and opposition. Or they follow the leaders, and leave.
>
> *The leavers,* the people who were threatening to leave, leave anyway. Many leave physically, they get up and go, others leave in their hearts, they just become passive-aggressive around anything the leader attempts to do.

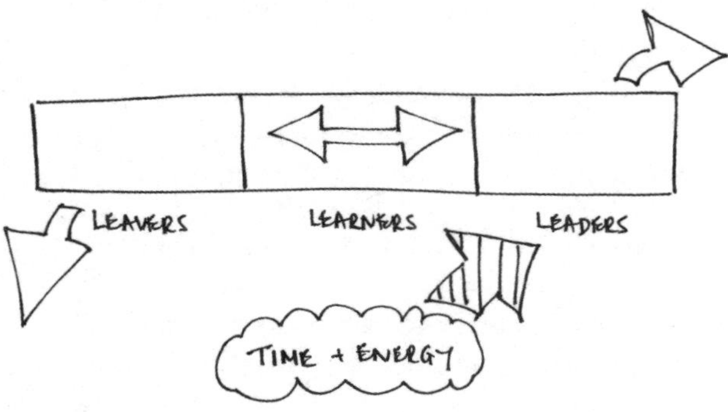

I determined very early in my ministry that I was going to give no oxygen to those who had resolutely decided that they didn't like me and didn't like my vision. I would give plenty of time and opportunity to people to decide whether they were in or out and even later would keep the door ajar, but it was not only a waste of my time but also a strategic leadership mistake to implicitly decide that my pioneers should leave, that I should create a culture of profound conservatism and deep cynicism and I should preside over a declining ministry.

You get to decide who is going to leave and who you are going to lead.

Leaders' reality check:

- Leader, you bear light – but you will have to walk through darkness. That is what light is for.
- Leader, you must have a plan – or the dream will not happen. But you will have to stick to it in the chaos – that's what a plan is for.
- Leader, you will build community and it will be beautiful. But for this to be, you must risk betrayal and loss – it comes with the territory.

It does for Jesus.
It does for Jesus-leaders.

When he had received the drink, Jesus said, 'It is finished.' With that, he bowed his head and gave up his spirit.

John 19

7.

SACRIFICE

So the soldiers took charge of Jesus. Carrying his own cross, he went out to the place of the Skull (which in Aramaic is called Golgotha). There they crucified him, and with him two others – one on each side and Jesus in the middle.

Pilate had a notice prepared and fastened to the cross. It read: JESUS OF NAZARETH, THE KING OF THE JEWS. Many of the Jews read this sign, for the place where Jesus was crucified was near the city, and the sign was written in Aramaic, Latin and Greek. The chief priests of the Jews protested to Pilate, 'Do not write "The King of the Jews", but that this man claimed to be king of the Jews.'

Pilate answered, 'What I have written, I have written.'

When the soldiers crucified Jesus, they took his clothes, dividing them into four shares, one for each of them, with the undergarment remaining. This garment was seamless, woven in one piece from top to bottom.

'Let's not tear it,' they said to one another. 'Let's decide by lot who will get it.'

This happened that the scripture might be fulfilled that said, 'They divided my clothes among them and cast lots for my garment.'

So this is what the soldiers did.

Near the cross of Jesus stood his mother, his mother's sister, Mary the wife of Clopas, and Mary Magdalene. When Jesus saw his mother there, and the disciple whom he loved standing nearby, he said to her, 'Woman, here is your son,' and to the disciple, 'Here is your mother.' From that time on, this disciple took her into his home.

Later, knowing that everything had now been finished, and so that Scripture would be fulfilled, Jesus said, 'I am thirsty.' A jar of wine vinegar was there, so they soaked a sponge in it, put the sponge on a stalk of the hyssop plant, and lifted it to Jesus' lips. When he had received the drink, Jesus said, 'It is finished.' With that, he bowed his head and gave up his spirit.

John 19:16b–30

The 1924 Olympic Games were to be held in Paris, France and a young American rower called Bill Havens had been chosen to represent the USA. He was faced with a massive decision. His pregnant wife was due to give birth at the same time as the Games. The choice: the opportunity to compete on sport's greatest stage or the birth of his child?[23]

Bill chose to stay.

He never won a gold medal. The sacrifice was considerable. To compound the issue, his younger brother Bud won three gold medals in other canoeing events that year.

Fast forward to 1952. The American favourite for the canoeing gold medal won the 10,000 canoeing singles in the Helsinki Olympics. He sent the following telegram to Bill Havens:

> 'Dear Dad, thanks for waiting around for me to get born in 1924. I'm coming home with the gold medal you should have won.
>
> Your loving son, Frank.'

The path to success goes through the valley of sacrifice. The way of the cross is the way of leadership in the kingdom of God.

You have to die in order to live.

At Caesarea Philippi, Peter and Jesus get into a discussion. Peter makes a declaration: 'You are the Messiah.' Jesus makes a promise: 'on this rock I will build my church, and the gates of Hades will not overcome it' (Matthew 16:16–18). It is a pivotal moment. Peter must have felt highly affirmed. Yet it is what happens next that interests us, and is at the heart of the maturing of the Jesus-leader. From then on Jesus goes to talk to his disciples about his death. But Peter takes him to one side and, we are told, 'began to rebuke him'. He rebukes God! Jesus says to him, 'Get behind me Satan!'

In other words, Peter, you are obstructing not only the plan of God, but the way of God.

---

[23] https://www.olympic.org/news/canoeist-havens-makes-his-father-proud

The plan of God and the way of God is the cross. There is no other way. Jesus begins to describe the way of the cross: 'Whoever wants to be my disciple must deny themselves and take up their cross and follow me. For whoever wants to save their life will lose it, but whoever loses their life for me will save it' (Matthew 16:21–25).

It is with this truth at their backs and those words in their ears that the disciples engage with the crucifixion and ultimately with their own calling.

THE WAY OF THE CROSS

At the climactic moment of Jesus' life, arguably of world history, is one word:

Tetelestai. It gets translated in English as, 'It is finished,' or 'It is accomplished,' or 'Done.' But it is one word, *tetelestai*.

Jesus spends his final breath in saying one word – for us, for those who listened then and for those who listen now. It is a victory cry at the moment of greatest loss. The very moment of loss provides the possibility for gain, for growth, for new life.

> *'unless a grain of wheat falls to the ground and dies, it remains only a single seed. But if it dies, it produces many seeds.'*
>
> John 12:24

The way of the cross declares that for life, real life, to be released, a death must be experienced.

If the goal of your leadership life is resurrection, new life, multiplication life, the pivotal point of your leadership life – the pivotal *points* of your leadership life – must be death.

Jesus is in agony hanging on a cross. He receives a drink from a sponge, a hyssop plant. He drinks, he speaks, he dies.

Finished?

For those standing around the cross, those who had shouted 'Crucify!' – probably the very same people as those who had shouted 'Hosannah!' – for them the meaning of *tetelestai* was clear.

If you were a servant you understood *tetelestai*. A servant would say to a master, '*Tetelestai*.' Which meant 'I've finished it, I've done what you asked me to do.' And he or she would expect to hear: 'Well done. It is finished.'

If you were a merchant, you would know what this word meant. A debt had been paid, and your receipt would have '*tetelestai*' stamped on it. It is finished, paid in full.

If you were an artist, or a craftsman, you would know what this word meant. You would step back from a piece that you had been working at for months, for years, and say '*Tetelestai*.' It is finished, and it is good, and it is excellent. (And you might do the 'thumb' thing.)

And if you were a priest, you would use this word, *tetelestai*, when someone had given a sacrifice that fulfilled all the requirements of the law, and you would pronounce: '*Tetelestai*.' It is finished, it is accepted, it is right.

Jesus is saying, 'I have done it, I've completed the picture, I've paid the price, I've dealt with the debt, I'm the perfect sacrifice. It is good, it is well, and it is finished. It is done.'

Scripture fulfilled

Jesus is saying that Scripture has been fulfilled. *Tetelestai*. There are stacks of specific fulfilments of Old Testament prophecy in this passage of Scripture: the soldiers divide Jesus' garments and cast lots for his clothing (Psalm 22:18); none of his bones were broken (Exodus 12:46); Jesus' side was pierced with a spear (Zechariah 12:10). In fact, there are over 600 Old Testament prophecies fulfilled in the New Testament account of Jesus' life and death. Jesus is completing the picture, he is saying it is done, everything that was prophesied of the Messiah has been fulfilled.

It's done, in him.

Sacrifice completed

Jesus is saying '*Tetelestai*.' The debt is paid, the sacrifice is completed.

The sacrifice was everything the law was about, central to Jewish life, it was everything the rabbis talked about and taught about, for generations. And yet the cost of sin was never fully paid. The priests were never allowed to sit down when they were on duty – the work of atoning for sin was never done, there was always more.[24]

So what Jesus is saying is that all of this system, all of this ritual, over generations, over hundreds of years, the animals, the blood, the altar stuff, it all gets its fulfilment in him.

Satan defeated

John describes the place that Jesus was crucified as 'Golgotha, the place of the skull.' Jesus deals with the problem of sin and death and hell at the place of the skull. When Jesus dies he wins victory over sin and death and hell, and the authority that has been wrested from us by Satan gets handed back. It's as if Jesus says, 'I'll have the keys to this world. I'll have the keys. All authority has now been given to me.' *Tetelestai.*

Salvation secured

And Jesus is saying salvation is secured, it is done, it is accomplished, *tetelestai*. Personal salvation for you and I. It's dealt with at the cross. The temple was torn in two signifying that we can have open access to a God who loves us and chooses us and created us and wants to save us. Jesus says, '*Tetelestai*.' It is done! You can have life in all its fullness.

- This salvation is regeneration. You and I are given new life in Jesus.
- This salvation is justification. You and I have been put right with our Father God.

---

[24] Hebrews 10:11, 12.

- This salvation is adoption. You and I have been included in the family of God.
- This salvation is sanctification. The word of God in our lives, cleaning us up and conforming us to the person of Jesus.

It is finished, it is accomplished, it's a done deal. *Tetelestai*!

It is rare to find a leader who not only starts well but finishes well. One who can, with confidence, cry '*Tetelestai!*'. I formulated a sentence in my mind, and then in my journal, that I would encourage you to complete.

At the end of my life I will be able to say 'Tetelestai' when …

It is accomplished, it is finished, but it needs finishing. Jesus sits down so that his followers can stand up and walk out their salvation and victory. The way of the cross. The way it gets finished is the way it got finished. The task is philosophically completed but experientially needs completing. The job of the leader is to finish the finished task. To press home the victory already won. The way it gets finished is the way it got finished.

So your ability to cry '*Tetelestai*' is dependent on your willingness to die. To live for *tetelestai* means you have to die well.

As I have studied Jesus-leaders, I have concluded that there are two significant moments in the life of the kind of leader that God loves.

- The moment that they realise what they are carrying.
- The moment that they lay it down.

The moment that you fully grasp who you are and what you are for and what you have been given to accomplish the task, you are powerful beyond belief. But the moment that you die, the moment that you surrender all to God and submit the stuff of your leadership dream to others is the secret to really living.

A fractal way

The way of the cross is not like some great climactic moment that you spend your whole life building up to, rather it is the culture and texture of the whole leadership journey. In every season there must be death if there is to be life. In fact, I sometimes wonder if, rather like a really frustrating computer game, leaders get stuck at certain levels, never able to graduate because they find themselves misunderstanding or unable to take the way of the cross. It is the only way to access the next part of the journey.

The way of the cross

THE WAY OF THE CROSS AND THE SEASONS OF A LEADERSHIP LIFE

A greater plan

God's plan is bigger and longer than your leadership life. Ironically, your ability to understand that will extend and lengthen the impact of your leadership. The leader's willingness to surrender to this greater plan is ultimately the making of that leader. William Booth, the founder of the Salvation Army, was once asked the secret to his success – he said this:

> I will tell you the secret – God has had all there was of me. There have been men with greater brains than I, men with greater opportunities, but from the day I got the poor of London on my heart and caught a vision of all Jesus Christ could do with them, on that day I made up my mind, that God would have all of William Booth there was. And if there is anything of power in the Salvation Army today it is because God has had all the adoration of my heart, all the power of my will, and all the influence of my life.[25]

Giving all of yourself is a form of dying. By the time that William Booth had physically died, it is estimated that more than 2 million people, most of them poor or suffering from addictions, had professed faith in Jesus. The key was not his physical death – but his continual leadership death.

A better strategy

The best way to live is to die. And the best way to gain is to give it away.

If it is true that you can't take anything with you when you die it is also true that you may as well give things away whilst you live. If, as I have asserted, dying should be a dynamic event in the life of a leader, and you die moment by moment as you lead – then the continual practice of giving away is also dynamic and is an aid to death.

What do you need to let go of?

What do you need to allow to die?

Apprentice leader

Perhaps this season is Autumn. It is a time of much activity, clearing ground and preparing soil for future growth. It is a season of hard work but it is the work of preparation.

What needs to die for life to come?

---

[25] Wayne E Warner, *1,000 Stories and Quotations of Famous People* (Baker Book House, 1972).

Jesus has already framed the characteristics of one who takes up the cross. They must deny themselves. This is a hard ask in a culture of rampant entitlement, a society where younger leaders tend to assume that they deserve recognition, status, rights or role. What does it look like if the measure becomes Jesus, the position becomes servant and the right is to die?

My first ministry role was working with an organisation called Oasis Trust. It was in the early years of gap year ministry positions, and, in the enthusiasm and arrogance of youth, I was excited to be leading a team in the east end of London. To be honest, I thought I was pretty much the perfect choice – I was passionate about Jesus, confident in my abilities and charismatic in my leadership. At the first weekend of training one of the speakers gave me a picture. He saw me walking into a cave with a host of people following and getting deeper and deeper into the cave until I was hemmed in and blocked – I'm a little claustrophobic so it wasn't a comfortable picture for me. At the back of the cave was a small hole that I didn't think I could get through but it was the only way out. And actually as hundreds of people had come into the cave it was the only way anyone was going to get out. It seemed that God was asking me to become small and to pull hundreds of people through after me – the point was obvious but the picture was poignant. When I stand large in my gifting, rights or role, I significantly limit my ability to lead the people God was calling me to lead. I had to make myself small.

Apprentice leader, so do you. To stand on your rights is a ridiculous concept in the kingdom of God.

What needs to die for the apprentice leader?

- Comfort needs to die. The desire for an easy life. What I signed up to was a hard life. The best job in all the world, but a job where death was the constant experience.
- Comparison needs to die. The desire to appraise my life up against any other lives. The temptation to jealousy and competition needs to die. Remember, you are The Project.

> Your wiring and calling is unique. Your development, its pace and content will be unique. Your challenges and your capacities will be unique. Die to comparison.

Remember, in the very act of taking up your sword of leadership in this Jesus movement you are pledging to lay it down.

The emerging leader

The season for the emerging leader may well be winter. It is the season of greatest growth, but that growth often happens hidden, unseen, under the surface. It is the season of strengthening, forming, shaping what will be, for the future. It is perhaps the most important season of a leader's life.

What needs to die in this season?

- The desire to be seen and noticed needs to die. This key season of growth in leadership happens best in hiddenness – most of the leadership examples we find in the Scriptures experienced times of training and equipping in the hidden places of this world. Jesus himself spent forty days in the wilderness, Paul probably spent three years in the Arabian desert. Moses was forty years in the backside of the desert and Joseph spent several years in prison. And all as preparation for significant leadership roles which were as yet unseen but emerging.
- Ambition needs to die. Don't emerge too soon. Don't shout before it is time. Don't publish your biography or your leadership lessons before you have learned them – live them. This is the time of your preparation. And hiddenness is a constant tool – in the preparation and development and armoury of the leader. Jesus constantly spent time alone with the Father. One of the significant dangers of my leadership journey is that as an extreme extrovert I run from hiddenness. So every lesson I learn is lived out in front of everyone else – but sometimes

Jesus has things to say that are not to be preached, that are just for me and for him, to prepare me for him. God has things for my heart and my soul which are not yet for anyone else. I am always wrestling with the hiddenness of the journey that God is calling me into.

- The love of the 'new thing' needs to die. The desire to discover the golden bullet of ministry that no one else has discovered, or the desire to jump on someone else's idea because it is trending in someone else's world, needs to die. I firmly believe that when all things are revealed, we will be shocked by our addiction to a quick fix gospel that grasps for superficial solutions. The tyranny of the golden bullet needs to die. It will keep you in crowd-pleasing alternatives to the deep plans of God.
- Future blinkers need to die. The desire to live and lead in the future has to die. You have to learn to lead in your season before you will ever be able to lead in the next. If your dreams and schemes and plans are always for a future moment you will never lead well now, you will never learn the lessons now that will equip you for the future that you dream of.

I'm at the age and stage where I now need varifocal glasses to preach with. They enable me to see near and far at the same time. I found that my reading glasses were fine for reading but disabled me in seeing anyone I was speaking to, it meant that I rarely used them, so I could see people but not really my notes. Preaching was becoming a better communication exercise for me but a less accurate articulation of my study time. So I went varifocal – so must you if you want to lead well. You will always want to see into the distance, that is good. But not at the expense of what God has for you now. The doorway to the future and a more productive season lies at the back end of a room called 'Lead what is in front of you.' At least it would be called that if the title wasn't so cumbersome.

Accomplished, seasoned leader

Perhaps this is the season of spring. Much of what was growing in the winter has now sprouted; many of the seeds sown in your life are producing a harvest; there is fruitfulness in your ministry and it is evident. You are now seen and noticed, and, irrespective of the size of your leadership, it is evident to people around that you are leading.

What still needs to die?

- Reputation needs to die. The moment that you believe your own hype is the moment of greatest danger for your legacy – the moment that you pay attention to your press, either negative or positive, is a time of serious danger for the success or failure of the thing that God has called you to. You see, ownership is not maturity. Maybe I'm being harsh but I'm always suspicious when leaders start to name ministries after themselves, buildings after themselves, when ministries that were built on giving it all away suddenly become ministries that are bringing it all in. The temptation in this season to claim it, own it, and name it as yours is large. You don't need to preserve or enhance your reputation. You know that, so don't.
- Consolidation needs to die. I have also seen innumerable senior leaders who started off with a pioneer calling stop short because they changed their perspective. I know gifted male and female leaders who know who they are and what they are for, forget, give up, lay it down and settle. The temptation to win a frontier and then just preserve what you have got is significant.

  Don't hear what I'm not saying.

  I'm not saying that that land taken doesn't need to be settled. But what I am saying is you can't begin to lead as if it is peacetime when it is actually still war. The culture of taking territory and the call to take land is not something that gets rescinded at a certain stage of ministry.

I am deeply concerned not to bequeath to my children the battles that were mine to fight, the territory that I should have taken, that was mine to take. They will have their own fights. Their own territory, their own victories to win – they don't need to clean up after me.

For the last two years Niki and I have been wrestling with the need to break a culture around leadership which is taking us on a faith journey. We have always lived in a tied house, a manse. And the manse that we live in now is a generous gift from the church and a beautiful place to live. It is used continually as a place where people can stay and a base for our ministry. But it is an old wineskin, a model that made sense in a previous generation but, as we plant churches all over Scotland, not a model that can be replicated. So, in our late forties Niki and I need to venture out again into unknown territory into a kingdom adventure, letting go of some security to make space for ourselves, for others, but above all for the purposes of God. We feel that if we don't fight that battle, we pass it on for someone else to fight. What we model is as important as what we say and do.

Sage

The season may well be summer. Summer is a season of rest and of celebration – where we gather with family and friends and enjoy the harvest that is being brought in.

What needs to die for the sage?

Perhaps the desire to freewheel down the mountain, having pedaled hard up, needs to die. Perhaps it's a traditional view of retirement that needs to die – as a lessening of responsibility, an absence of work and an abdication of the call. Rather, retirement might be seen as a change of pace and a change of posture.

Your activity is not frenetic, it is focused. You may not go to people, but they will come to you. Your strength is in story and experience, and not in activity and accomplishment. Your home may become your biggest spiritual weapon. Your story becomes your greatest bequest.

Tell your hero story. With all its flaws. It will inspire other hero stories. Many hero stories. Write it down, speak it out, publish it widely. Those who follow need your wisdom, your glory and your pain.

I see spiritual leaders who can quote day, week, month hour to the moment they retire. Stop freewheeling down the mountain. This season may be a season to die to control. Let go of the life you once led. Release the people that once served you. And allow the communities and the relationships space to dictate their orbits with you. There is a generation rising that needs you to become grandparent, consultant, mentor, and to finish well.

The writer to the Hebrews tells us that Jesus sat down (Hebrews 10:12); he had finished, he had accomplished. He sat down at the right hand of the Father, in a place of authority, but he sat down. The season of sage is a season to sit down, to write your experiences and tell your story and open your home and your life. And finish well.

My friend Jim has finished well. He is in his mid-eighties and as I write this is in the very last moments of his life. Jim has been a giant amongst the leaders of God's people. His way has been the way of the cross. Through toils and snares he has modelled, taught and encouraged God's people to be disciples of word and spirit. He has known loss but he has died well. For the last twenty years, in a season that the world around him would call retirement, he has been more active and more fruitful than perhaps in any other season of his life. Encouraging church renewal, supporting Christian leaders and speaking into my life. I would love to be able to listen in to the applause of heaven as God the Father, God the Son and God the Holy Spirit say, 'Well done, good and faithful servant,' to Jim.

The way of the cross is the only way of success for the leader.

At the end of my life, I will be able to cry *'Tetelestai!'* when …

8.

SUCCESSION

Jesus said to her, 'Mary.'

She turned towards him and cried out in Aramaic, 'Rabboni!' (which means 'Teacher').

Jesus said, 'Do not hold on to me, for I have not yet ascended to the Father. Go instead to my brothers and tell them, "I am ascending to my Father and your Father, to my God and your God."'

Mary Magdalene went to the disciples with the news: 'I have seen the Lord!' And she told them that he had said these things to her.

On the evening of that first day of the week, when the disciples were together, with the doors locked for fear of the Jewish leaders, Jesus came and stood among them and said, 'Peace be with you!' After he said this, he showed them his hands and side. The disciples were overjoyed when they saw the Lord.

Again Jesus said, 'Peace be with you! As the Father has sent me, I am sending you.' And with that he breathed on them and said, 'Receive the Holy Spirit. If you forgive anyone's sins, their sins are forgiven; if you do not forgive them, they are not forgiven.'

John 20:16–23

In a very old church in West Yorkshire, Blackley Baptist Church, there are some wonderful plaques and tablets on the walls. One reads:

> In grateful appreciation of the services and gifts of James Cartledge esq., who founded this church in 1789 and preached **for a few years** until a pastor was appointed.

Another reads:

> Reverend John Rigby whose wise leadership, Christian counsel and faithful preaching were **largely** owned by God during his pastorate of the Church.

The best, however, is the plaque on the communion table which reads:

> To the Glory of God and in loving appreciation of the faithful service presented to Blackley Baptist Church by the ladies' sewing class 1917 and to commemorate faithful services rendered to this church by **Annie and Betty**, faithful **wives** of Reverend Briggs, Pastor, 1874–1910.

What will be written about you? What will be your legacy? Will you live for something that will outlast you? Or will you settle for pursuing and living for your own success?

Success or Succession? I'm not sure that you can have both.

BEYOND-YOU LEADERSHIP

The leadership commission that we witness, as we read these verses of Scripture, is surrounded by, and grounded in, the reality of a miraculous resurrection. Jesus is alive – the future is bright and certain.

This commission has us reaching forward and beyond. We are called to die well but we are called to look for resurrection. We lead in a world where we constantly experience death but hope for eternal life. The call is to lead, laying down our lives that those very lives might be ramps for the leadership beyond us – the leadership of others.

The problem is that much of our motivation is still fundamentally selfish. It's *all* about you. *Your* leadership. *Your* legacy. *Your* memory. *Your* mark on the world. *Your* dent in the universe. Jesus models a 'beyond-you' leadership.

Jesus meets Mary Magdalene and, encouraging and releasing her, he appoints her as his first evangelist. Allow me to pause here. Don't miss the staggering importance of this moment.

Jesus appears first to Mary.
A woman.

This is beautifully offensive. The excluded becomes entrusted, the marginalised takes centre stage. Jesus totally levels the playing field.

The story of the role of women in redemptive history has been building towards this point, through Deborah and Huldah and Mary the Christ-bearer. It's going to move on to include Philip's prophesying daughters, and Junia and Priscilla. Jesus' ministry was full of strong female leaders and was funded by strong female leaders. Now he sends Mary, the first human to carry the gospel. The first to see him risen from the dead, the first herald, preacher, evangelist. He gives to a woman, who is not allowed anywhere near the key parts of the temple, nowhere near the presence of God, the responsibility of being an apostle to the apostles.

Leader, I am absolutely convinced that the unshackled flourishing of female leadership in your community is a sign and a symbol of the heart of the kingdom at hand. I am so proud of the female leaders raised up from within the church that I lead. I am proud of and jealous for the potential in my wife, my daughters and my many sisters called of God to lead. I see an army of women, apostles, prophets, disciples, leaders, business women and artists, leading like Jesus and scaring the hell out of hell.

Here Jesus meets Mary Magdalene. His strong message to her is 'Don't cling on to me' (v. 17) – but rather give me away.

Don't hold on, pass it on.

Then he comes to his disciples through a locked door into a fearful room: his message is 'Peace.' Peace for them and peace through them. He ministers with grace and truth to Thomas the skeptic. This is the culmination of a three-year apprenticeship programme in which Jesus has been catalyst, coach, challenger and champion.

- Catalyst – example, model
- Coach – support, equip, encourage
- Challenger – permit, release, critique
- Champion – relational cheerleader

Jesus now commissions the disciples to do the same. To lead beyond themselves, for something bigger than them, for leaders who will succeed them and for a dream beyond them.

He commissions his leaders to a 'beyond-you' leadership, 'As the Father has sent me, I am sending you.' He breathes on them and they receive the Holy Spirit, 'If you forgive anyone's sins, their sins are forgiven. If you do not forgive them, they are not forgiven.' (John 20:21–23). It's an incredible statement.

Same style,
same appointing,
same call,
same anointing,
same authority,
same results,
… as Jesus.

The same perspective, the same scope, the same trajectory. Beyond you.

My father, who baptised me, gave me, as he prayed for me, John 15:16, 'You did not choose me but I chose you and appointed you so that you might go and bear fruit – fruit that will last'. That is my call, that is what I hold in my heart, that is what I whisper in the moments that I want to quit. That beyond-me call, that 'fruit that will last' call, is the thing I remind my soul of when I am tempted to bow to the opinion of others or live for their applause. A beyond-me call. It began with him and belongs to him and outlives me.

A beyond-you vision

Jesus, is going to expand on this commission. As he leaves the earth he says to his bewildered disciples that his Spirit will propel them and the message they carry, not just into Jerusalem and Judea (close to them and quite like them), but onto Samaria and the ends of the earth (beyond them).

If your vision is not beyond you, your purpose will be about you, your team will only serve you and your dream will die with you. If your vision is not beyond you, it is dependent on you and limited by you.

> In reality, it is a to-do list.
> In all probability, it is disappointing to God.

Many leaders talk about vision, when what they mean is 'a plan', one that is limited by them, their abilities, their capacities, their imaginations and their lifetimes. Jesus' resurrection offers more. Jesus' commission is beyond.

A beyond-you focus

There was one moment in my ministry when God seemed to say to me,

> 'What you are doing is not very good.'

And it didn't make much sense, because I thought what I was doing was, by most measures, pretty good. I had a growing, youthful and passionate church. We had grown from a church of about 180, and we were at that time about 700 people. And so I had this argument with God. I said, 'Well I think it is.

I know you're usually right. But on this occasion … I beg to differ.'

And he said to me, 'What you are growing is a mile wide and an inch deep. You are one smoke machine away from a mega church … (he didn't use that exact language, that's me) … but actually this is not what I'm doing.'

So I started to investigate discipleship and missional communities. And I discovered something which has been very significant for me.

What I began to see was that Jesus was amazing in every social space. He was awesome with the crowd. I mean there was nobody like Jesus in communication with the crowd. Check it out – check out the Sermon on the Mount. He was awesome. He was amazing with the seventy-two. I mean look at how he sends them out: it's an incredible passage of Scripture. He was at his best with the twelve and the three, but he always wanted to be with the Father.

Now here's the interesting thing. There is a journey that's being made, always: watch it. Jesus was always trying to get away from the crowd to the seventy-two, away from the seventy-two to the twelve, away from the twelve to the three and away from the three to the One.

And the Lord said to me, 'Karl, why are you always trying to make the opposite journey?' And I think probably it's what most church leaders do.

One leader with a thousand followers sounds great, but the influence will last, at most, a lifetime. It will make a seasonal splash. But a leader who grows a thousand leaders – who each grow a thousand more – can change the world.

This is Jesus-leadership. If you have a vision that is beyond you, you can set a purpose that is beyond you. A beyond-you purpose means that what you begin to build may well be completed after you have gone. And more, what you develop should be built upon as a foundation when your leadership tenure is past. A beyond-you purpose means that those you lead will surpass you, supersede you and eclipse you. A beyond-you purpose results in those you lead not always serving your dream but developing and running with theirs. They may well leave you. And that's a good thing!

A beyond-you leadership requires that those you currently lead are free to make their own mistakes because you have modelled transparent success and failure to the extent that they will not make your mistakes. Your success becomes their springboard and your train wrecks become their schooling.

So how do you do succession?

Focus

Healthy succession requires focus. My experience in leadership tells me that business and driven-ness, unless intentionally harnessed in a beyond-me direction, will always suffocate a beyond-me purpose. I will have no time or patience for succession and I will trade it for superficial and short-term success. This is not Jesus. Should he have so chosen, Jesus could have done a pretty good solo job, but he knew something that we will understand only if we pause long enough to consider.

The primary function of leadership is not to attract followers but to lead leaders.

This is often quoted but rarely walked out. Jesus knew that if something was worth doing, it was worth doing averagely by successors, rather than doing brilliantly by himself. Leader, I know it is a tough teaching, but your competency, efficiency and brilliance at doing the thing that God has gifted you to do, could well be the very thing that is killing the thing that God has called you to do. Your calling is to lead, and that call is beyond you, so you must make space.

'No' is your strongest weapon. Use it. Say 'No' to good so that you can say 'Yes' to best.

For succession to be successful there has to be a relational process. Those I apprentice orbit around my family and my house and become my friends. Anything that is going to become a movement must be built relationally. If you get to the end of the process of releasing those who will succeed you and the relationship is still held together by structure, you have not done it Jesus' way and it is unlikely to last.

Who are your three?

If Jesus was always making a journey from the crowd to the three, most leaders spend most of our time trying to make the opposite journey: from the three through the twelve and seventy-two to the crowd. Not only is this not the way of kingdom succession, it doesn't work! If you want a crowd, you don't get one by trying to get a crowd – you get one by building into the three.

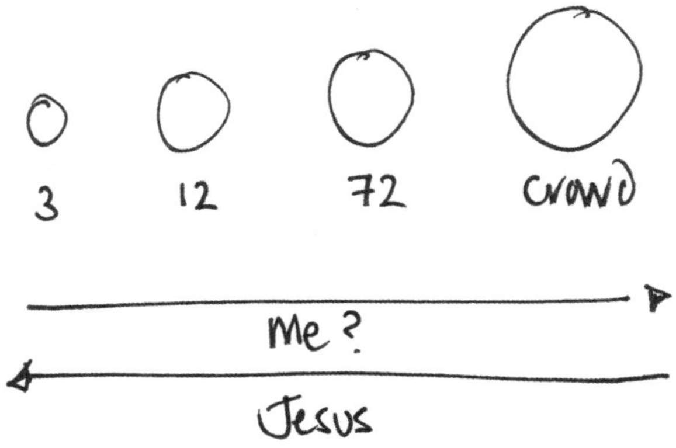

We've already looked at how Jesus invested in the twelve, his *talmidim* (see p xxxi), and how the disciples walked in his dust, but it seems to me the real genius of Jesus' plan is his apprenticeship of the three. It is Peter, James and John who get the most direct input from the head of the church and it is they who end up leading the fledgling church. Peter, and then James in Jerusalem, and then John in Ephesus (possibly *the* most significant centre in the early church movement), as far as we can make out, end up leading the most significant centres in the early church movement.

Who are your three?
What do they need?

Your leadership call is to love everyone you lead, but invest unequally. Everyone you lead has equal value, but not equal time from you. The success of your beyond-you call is dependent on your spending more time with fewer people. You will have apprentices – not favourites. Prioritising your three and your twelve will not make you popular but it will secure your legacy and build a movement.

Who are your three?
Your twelve?
Your seventy-two?
What do they need?

FOUR STEPS TO HEALTHY SUCCESSION

For healthy succession to occur, your three, and your twelve, need you to be catalyst, coach, challenger and champion. All four.

- Catalyst
- Coach
- Challenger
- Champion

Catalyse

Building a succession, rather than just being a success, demands that you find your voice. Those you lead need to hear your dream.

This Jesus-leadership is an audacious dream. It is light for people and light for darkness. It is restoration for all things and it is salvation for all people. 'Come follow me – I will make you fishers of men' (Matthew 4:19 NIV 1984). 'The time has come, … the kingdom of God has come near. Repent and believe the good news!' (Mark 1:15).

Leadership that has no dream is essentially myopic. It is short-sighted and narrow-minded and leads people nowhere. When God raises unlikely people and helps them find their voice, he always gives them a dream. And this is vital. Because the dreams that leaders have, and the way in which they find their voice, pours oil on the troubled waters of the fears that followers have. Fears that disable them in living life and enjoying light.

So find your voice. Find your visionary voice. That's what made Martin Luther King such an incredible leader – he was able to articulate what was on his heart. In 1963, when he marched to the Washington monument with hundreds of thousands of black men and women to place his stake in the ground around equality and rights for all people, he began with a speech which by every reckoning was dull and predictable. Midway through the speech from somewhere behind him, Marsalia Jackson, one of Martin's biggest supporters, called, 'Tell them about the dream, Martin.' You see, Martin Luther King had a dream, and he had articulated it in many places at many times. It had become mundane to him and he had resolved not to speak of it, but Marsalia Jackson ignited something in him, helped him find his voice, and his voice changed the world.

I have a dream.
So do you.
What is it?

Craft it.
Give it voice.
Don't ever stop speaking it.
May your dream always be beyond, outrageous, out of reach.

Every vision I have ever articulated to the church at Central has been ridiculous – they've been visions that we could not do and which usually freaked me out. Most recently, we have gone on record with a dream for the transformation of our nation and the re-evangelisation of Europe through the Celtic lands. And we have given ourselves twenty years to establish a hundred centres of mission in the key towns and cities of the Celtic lands.[26] We are asking God for one million people to come to know Jesus. Currently, we have a great church of about a thousand people, a couple of church plants and a number of really keen young leaders. That's a big God gap. It's just ridiculous enough to work.

Many inspirational leaders catalyse well. They are great starters. They gather followers and energy around their vision, then perhaps delegate but eventually frustrate because there is no real release mechanism for succeeding leadership. It creates a one-generational leadership culture and only helps the intuitively gifted, high functioning apprentice. If all you do is cast vision, you will create a culture of frustration in which followers will grow disillusioned and potentially take matters into their own hands. Dreams will be birthed too soon and have limited chance to grow in a healthy way.

The best that catalysts can do is inspire. This is not enough.

Healthy succession is dependent not only on the ability to inspire but also to empower. The engine room of true apprenticeship is fuelled and managed by coaches and challengers. They are the leaders who intentionally spend time honing gift, developing character and growing dreams. At their best, coaches and challengers empower others.

---

[26] www.cairnmovement.com

Coach

Those you apprentice and coach are going to need two things from you:

Face

Show it.

Jesus didn't dazzle from a distance, he discipled in the dirt. Those who follow need proximity and time to grow into their call. They are not looking for distant or virtual leadership. What they need is life on life. My life, like yours, is incredibly busy. But this is the vital work of a beyond-you leader. Those you are apprenticing need your time.

So open your diary to them and open your home to them. You don't need to add a huge number of extra meetings to your schedule, just cheat a little.

If I am travelling, I may as well travel with someone else, I must eat lunch, but I don't need to eat it alone, I will be preparing talks but there is no reason why someone can't be with me as I do so. In order to release a new generation of leaders, you don't have to become busier but you may need to prioritise and you must become smarter.

Pace

Slow it.

Niki and I run. Separately.

We do almost everything together in life but I think we might be in real danger of marital trouble if we ran together. It's a pace issue. My legs are longer and I run faster, I pound the streets as if they need to pay for something they did to me. Niki has a more genteel, some might say 'windmill' action going on! I run ahead and then come back to support her. This apparently irritates Niki to the point of distraction. We don't run together. It's a pace issue. And so is your beyond-you leadership. Those you lead will not run at your pace, not yet. They need you to be a pacemaker. Many will need you to slow down, to dial back, to explain what you are doing and why, so that they can understand and replicate. Writing this book is part of the discipline of grace: slowing down to articulate why and why not, how and how not, what and what not, and when. If all you ever show your followers are end results, successes or failures, they will just make the same mistakes you made. Apprentices need to be close enough and valued enough to sit in on debate, to hear your thinking, to see your own re-works. This is the stuff of coaching.

Remember the square we drew at the start, in *Set*? Those you apprentice need you to go both ways around it.

They need you to dial back from your unconscious competence to your conscious competence. They need you to work out why you do what you do and how you do it, so they can do it as well, only better. They need to hear your stories, they need you to write your book, they need you to give your perspective.

Many of the younger leaders you lead will not have the same capacity as you, not yet. They will not be able to carry the same load that you carry, not yet. You need to pace yourself. Equally you may need to help others pace themselves if they want a lifetime of leadership. One of the smartest pieces of advice I was given by a senior leader as they assessed my leadership style, was for me to go and find something to do that was not my job, that I could put intensity and focus into. He saw that I was killing my team with the pace I was running at and the intensity of my work life. My place is the golf course and my goal is a single figure handicap. Pars and birdies might just save some burnout for others and for me.

To be a great leader, you must learn to be a great coach, but you must not stay *only* a coach. If you sit too long in the coach's seat you will likely create a culture of dependence. It's the dark side of coaching. If you create an environment of protection for too long, or a culture of support too strong, those you lead begin to need you and depend on you and never grow the leadership muscles they need to walk into their destinies. You must help them stretch.

Challenge

Jesus was a challenger. To Peter, 'On you I will build my church and the gates of hell will not prevail against it.' To all his followers, 'If anyone would come after me – he must deny himself, take up his cross and follow me'. Before the commissioning, Jesus meets Mary. He sends her, saying, 'Do not hold on to me'.[27] She wanted to be with him, but he wants to send her. They want to be with you – you must send them. You must help them stretch.

As I train up and release leaders, my sole aim is to raise up Jesus-leadership. This is clearly not possible in my own strength or in my own ability. I will always be, at best, a pale reflection of him. I have to leave a God gap. A space that cannot be filled by my wisdom and experience, or the apprentice's ability and

---

[27] Matthew 17:18, my paraphrase; Matthew 16:18, 24; John 20:17.

potential. For their leadership to really be Jesus-leadership and to have the same impact as Jesus, it must be empowered by Jesus. I want to raise apprentices, who lead leadership lives that demand supernatural explanation. So I have to intentionally create God gaps for myself and for my team.

A budget that I can fully fund, without prayer and a miracle, is not a beyond-me budget and won't raise up beyond-me leaders. A plan that I can totally manage and skilfully execute is not a beyond-me plan and won't raise up kingdom-minded and faith-filled leaders.

An intrinsic part of our discipleship boot camps is a weekly challenge which is designed to create a God gap and put emerging leaders in a place of dependency. Whether their task is to share faith, pray for the sick, give away all their money or some other crazy scheme, the idea is to create a space where, if God does not show up, they will fall flat on their faces.

A regular activity of our staff team is to go onto the streets and speak to the 98% of people in our city who don't know Jesus. Scott, who is the key evangelist in my team, often wheels out a sofa onto the street and just sits down. Over a thousand people pass by the front of the church building every hour. Some stop and sit down – more than you would think – and some of them come to faith. Scott is taking apprentices with him, showing faith, stretching faith.

To be a challenger you are going to need GRACE. Grow it.

You will need to develop grace for failure and grace for mediocrity and patience for having a go, if you would see success and excellence in the long term.

The face plant and the easy win

There are very few things more embarrassing or indeed more painful than public failure. Equally, however, given the right environment and the right perspective, there are very few things that will grow you faster and stronger than failing and doing it obviously. Other leadership writers have talked about 'failing forward'.[28] It's a powerful perspective.

If you are reading this in a European context, listen very carefully. The prevalent leadership culture is that failure is always, always seen in a negative light. Which means people really struggle to learn from it. Leaders are tempted to hide failure, forget it, or ignore it, because so many carry the scars, and have known the pain of those moments and decisions that have become the identity of their leadership life.

But your face plant can grow you.

The Apostle Peter grew from his failed tent suggestion on the Mount of Transfiguration; from his 'you shall never wash my feet' in the upper room and from his 'I don't even know him' around the fire in the courtyard,[29] to be the wise one who is able to lead the church and write 'though now for a little while you may have had to suffer grief in all kinds of trials. These have come so that the proven genuineness of your faith – of greater worth than gold … may result in praise, glory and honour …'[30]

As we apprentice younger leaders at Central, we often have to encourage failure. A number of the high achievers who come around the church have never learned to fail well and consequently experience limited growth until they do. I remember encouraging one of our apprentices, who had pretty much succeeded in everything she had attempted throughout her young life (she was and is a pretty brilliant individual), that my best accomplishment over the year would be to help her fail well, on my watch, in the safety of the Father's house. In fact, I was going to put her in situations that would expose her in order to grow her. She now takes more risks and has grown to be a seasoned risk-taking leader of God's people.

Develop an environment where failure is not only accepted as part of life, or even a necessary evil of growing, but rather is the way in which we all learn and is therefore to be celebrated.

---

28 John C Maxwell, *Failing Forward: Turning Mistakes into Stepping Stones for Success* (Thomas Nelson, 2007).

29 Matthew 17:1–8; John 13:8; John 18:17, 25, 27, my paraphrase.

30 1 Peter 1:6–7.

If you are the senior leader or gatekeeper in your organisation this is on you.

In the church I lead, we are careful to applaud those who had a go and didn't initially succeed, as much as we tell the good news stories of those who 'knocked the ball out of the park'. One of the very first missional communities we launched realised after about a year that it really wasn't working, so, after trying to help them recalibrate, we agreed that they should stop. As part of the process, and to model a healthy perspective on leadership, we invited the team to be prayed for as they closed down. We did this publicly, with no embarrassment, applauded them all and tried a different approach next time around. One of the leaders of that 'failed' group now leads another missional community and is preparing to lead a team to plant a church in another city.

'If something is worth doing, it's worth doing badly' may sound like a really bad idea, until it is explained properly – then it sounds like just the right idea. How will anyone learn if they don't have a shot? My experience is that it then, very quickly, feels like a bad idea again when you have to live with the fallout of inexperienced and sometimes downright bad leadership choices.

You will need grace. Your younger leaders will need to fail and fall and learn and grow and make a mess on your watch, with your reputation on the line and with your relational and leadership capital exposed and vulnerable. But that's what it takes to lead in a beyond-you style.

Remember, if you grow entrepreneurs, almost never will their first idea and their first attempt be right: it just won't – it's a prototype, not yet right. The second attempt will be more likely halfway right and only by the third will they have something worth doing. It's a process, a process that you cannot shortcut or truncate if you would grow leaders well.

Let them have a go, expect them to fail.
Champion them.
Defend them.

Clean up the mess.
Applaud them. And start the process again.

They need you to believe in them, even when they are not the finished article. They need you to advocate for them, even when you know they might disappoint, because there will come a day when they will not disappoint but make you proud. They need you to take a punt on them even when the odds appear long.

Who do you need to push?
Where do you need to see failure?
How do you do this with grace?

And take care – remember the dark side of challenge is domination and abuse. If all you do is challenge, you will create a culture of fear and insecurity. You also need to grow through the stages of catalyst, coach and challenger to become a champion.

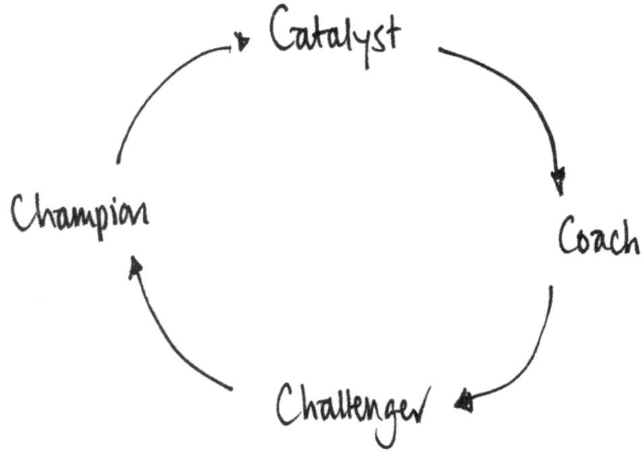

Champion

To champion is to operate with relational influence – you may have no functional leadership role, but you are still leading.

From a distance. You are there to advise when asked, you are there to encourage when asked.

You are not there.
You need to develop SPACE.
You must grow your ability to be absent well.

You cast a shadow as a leader. Whether you think that shadow is big or small is not the issue. Your shadow is significant. Your shadow has a protecting function, it covers and it shields and it protects and that is really good … but it can also *over*shadow. You can intentionally or unintentionally stifle the very anointing that you are trying to release. You must know how to get out of the way. Jesus did. In fact, not only did he send the disciples out two by two, but as he leaves this world he tells his followers that it is a very good thing: 'it is for your good that I am going away. Unless I go away, the Advocate will not come to you'.[31] Jesus seems to suggest that his stepping out of the way ushers in a new reality that is better for everyone concerned and he was proved right.

What works for Jesus might just work for us, yet we tend to find it hard to step out of the way. Often this is for noble and pastoral reasons, we don't want those who follow to lose out or be damaged in the process of transition. Sometimes, however our motives are darker and more selfish and come out of a place of self-preservation: 'If I give it away, what will I have?', 'If I step out of the way, I will lose out.' It is a common and understandable response but it is not the way of the kingdom of God.

In the kingdom, if you try and keep it, you will lose it, if you give it away it will come back to you.[32] If you do yourself out of a job, you will always have a job, but if you hang on to a role you will lose your role. I see this all the time. Churches that don't know how to do succession plans and leaders who stay

---

[31] Luke 10; John 16:7.
[32] Matthew 10:39 and 16:25.

longer than they should. I heard someone say recently that the first order of business for a new leadership tenure should be a well-thought-out succession plan. It sounds crazy, I know, but it's a Jesus strategy.

I have in the top drawer of my desk a sealed envelope. The Plan. If I should die, who could lead the church and the movement. As dramatic as it seems, you should have one too: you have a last will and testament with a plan for your kids and this is your family too.

Make space.

Now I only come around the office and have face-to-face meetings with my team on two days in the week. Intentionally. What I discovered was that my presence in the building too often was becoming disabling to the growth and development of my team. When I was absent, leaders just got on with making the decisions they were more than capable of making – but when I was present, they knocked on my door and double checked. Your younger leaders need your absence.

Ban a CC culture. I am tired of emails that I don't need to see, but I was copied in because people were frightened to take a punt, have a go, make a call. Ban the culture, no CCs. If your emerging leaders are always covering their backs, they are not moving forward with confidence. They never fly until they are pushed out of the nest.

Where do you need to absent yourself?

Tim

Tim was a student in Edinburgh full of vision, passion and enthusiasm for the gospel and ministry. All floppy-haired and charity-shop-clothed, he led a student ministry he called *Movement*. He brought *Movement* around the church and the relationship started. It quickly became clear that I was as attracted to his vision and dreams as he was to mine. Tim became an apprentice, not just of the church, but of mine. And Tim grew quickly.

Coaching was a challenge with Tim because in many ways he was smarter than me, was quick to learn. I spent time pushing him on, and intentionally holding him back, because leadership muscles were growing but they were young and unproven. Tim went from being an apprentice to having a staff position in the church. I watched him grow from a hesitant and awkward communicator to a confident and sophisticated preacher. I watched him growing in understanding of his personality and the effect, both positive and negative, that it had on other leaders. And I have tracked his progress, at times in proximity and at other times with intentional distance, and with great joy, as I have seen him develop into a first class leader of God's people.

There was a significant moment for Tim when it became clear that he needed space. He needed to run with his dream now, and no longer serve mine. Not that the two were in conflict, but that for Tim to fly, he needed to get some airspace.

Space from me.

Space from the place where he had grown and freedom to become the leader that he needed to become. My role had shifted from coach and challenger to champion. I now speak to Tim when he wants to speak to me – any influence I have is only relational.

The relationship between Tim and I was never strained, but the seasoned leader, like a seasoned parent, can interpret the relational tensions and provocative visions of a younger leader – not as rebellious dishonour but as the natural stretching and yearning of the apostolic call. The seasoned leader makes space before space is taken. Tim left with blessing and ended up in a very successful national ministry and now is in training to lead a church. The gift of space is really important because space taken and vision grasped out of a spirit of rebellion usually ends badly.

My prayer and my call is that there may be many Tims – and Hannahs and Heathers and Thomases. Sons and daughters who stand on my shoulders and eclipse my successes. And then make space for others.

Make it your prayer, because it is your call also.

'Do you love me? . . '

'Feed my sheep . . . '

'Follow me! . . '

John 21

9.

SHEPHERD

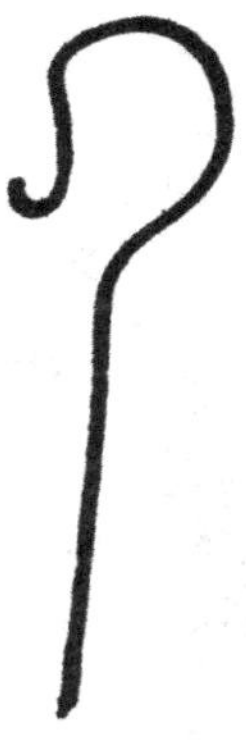

When they had finished eating, Jesus said to Simon Peter, 'Simon son of John, do you love me more than these?'

'Yes, Lord,' he said, 'you know that I love you.'

Jesus said, 'Feed my lambs.'

Again Jesus said, 'Simon son of John, do you love me?'

He answered, 'Yes, Lord, you know that I love you.'

Jesus said, 'Take care of my sheep.'

The third time he said to him, 'Simon son of John, do you love me?'

Peter was hurt because Jesus asked him the third time, 'Do you love me?' He said, 'Lord, you know all things; you know that I love you.'

Jesus said, 'Feed my sheep. Very truly I tell you, when you were younger you dressed yourself and went where you wanted;

but when you are old you will stretch out your hands, and someone else will dress you and lead you where you do not want to go.' Jesus said this to indicate the kind of death by which Peter would glorify God. Then he said to him, 'Follow me!'

John 21:15–19

•

The Lord is my shepherd, I shall not be in want.
He makes me lie down in green pastures,
he leads me beside quiet waters,
he restores my soul.
He guides me in paths of righteousness
for his name's sake.
Even though I walk
through the valley of the shadow of death,
I will fear no evil,
for you are with me;
your rod and your staff,
they comfort me.
You prepare a table before me
in the presence of my enemies.
You anoint my head with oil;
my cup overflows.
Surely goodness and love will follow me
all the days of my life,
and I will dwell in the house of the LORD
forever.

Psalm 23 (NIV 1984)

Shepherds in Scotland today ride quad bikes – which just changes things for me. What in my mind was once a lonely and desolate calling, usually located on the windswept and mist-draped uplands of some cold frontier, suddenly went high-tech and pretty cool.

It's always been cool to God. Reading the Scriptures carefully can lead to no other conclusion – God has a preference for shepherds, and when it comes to describing leadership, shepherding is the primary metaphor he employs.

Abel, whose offering was preferred over Cain's, was a shepherd. Abraham was a shepherd, albeit a pretty wealthy one, as were Moses and David. Jesus not only describes himself as 'the good shepherd' but is described by the writer to the Hebrews as being 'the great shepherd of the sheep' and indeed by Peter himself.[33]

To lead is to shepherd.

FISH OR LAMB?

Jesus is risen from the dead, and he has told his disciples to meet him 'up north' in Galilee. Peter is there. I imagine that he is confused and conflicted. He has just been a key player in the greatest event in the history of our world, but he has played a role that brings him only shame. He has denied that he knows Jesus, has shamed his master and potentially nullified his leadership call. And yet, Jesus had risen.

What do you do with all that?

Peter does the only thing he knows – he goes fishing. And, being still a leader, others follow, others go with him. Having caught nothing during the night, and knowing that they would catch nothing during the day, they make to return to shore, demoralised. It is now that Jesus meets with Peter, restores him and refashions his leadership call. Peter's trade is fisherman but

---

[33] John 10:11; Hebrews 13:20; 1 Peter 5:4.

his vocation is about to become shepherd … and so is yours. And so is mine.

Jesus meets Peter and feeds him – he cooks him breakfast. A variety of things are happening on a number of levels here. Jesus is clearly taking Peter back to the place of his greatest failure (including the detail of a charcoal fire) so that he can begin the process of healing and restoration. But, more than this, I think Jesus is shepherding Peter. Jesus feeds a hungry Peter, before he ever addresses Peter's restoration. No good leader asks a hungry man an important question before feeding him.

I have heard it said in a number of leadership conversations that a leader must do the right thing and only then pastor it, because too many leaders pursue the 'pastoral thing' and then try and make it right, which never works. I try to own this principle in leadership – I would never have changed anything, shifted thinking or transformed culture if I had prioritised making sure people felt 'pastored' above doing the right thing. Jesus is more concerned with truly loving people by setting his face towards the cross and rising again, and allowing Peter to go through the pain and learning of denial and restoration, more than he is concerned for Peter's comfort. But now that those things have been secured and won, he gives himself afresh to Peter's care. At no stage did the pioneer of our faith stop being the pastor of our hearts. But his leadership in this great venture necessitated doing the right thing above the pastoral thing. Indeed, when you truly do the right thing it is the pastoral thing. The leader, after doing the 'right thing', must shepherd, must pastor the flock!

Your vocation is shepherd.

You will not shepherd well unless you know what it is to be shepherded.

The great shepherd of the sheep is always wanting to shepherd his flock, his leaders, but you have to let him. He wants to meet us in the places we have retreated to. For Moses, as he shepherded, it was the 'backside of the desert' (KJV); for Elijah, as he ran for his life, it was 'the mountain of the Lord';[34] for Peter, it was a familiar boat and a familiar occupation.

In the place of the absence of clear direction, he wants to shepherd you.
In the desperate need for real restoration, he wants to shepherd you.
In the place of aching hunger and deep thirst, he wants to shepherd you.
But you need to let him.

He longs to meet you, but he waits for you to come to him. I know the very real temptation when at my lowest in leadership, when I feel abandoned, and not up to the task, when I start looking over the fence at everyone else's perfect life and search the web for any 'easier' job, to start to try to dig myself out, when all I need is shepherding.

Let him shepherd you.

But how?

Let him lay you down

According to David's famous description of God the shepherd, first you let him lay you down:

'He makes me lie down' (Psalm 23:2).

You stop trying to run as fast as you can. Let him lay you down.

One of the most obvious and acceptable leadership sins is busy, driven, over-achievement. I am seriously overqualified to write about this as I have many years of experiencing its fever and allowing others to deal with its fallout. It is the most invidious of sins, it appears noble but it is deeply prideful and totally destructive.

Leader, let him shepherd you, let him lay you down.

---

[34] Exodus 3:1; 1 Kings 19:8, 'the mountain of God'.

Let him lay you down. Or you will fall down. And you will let other people down.

- Take ten minutes a day to stop – stop everything – don't speak – don't act – just allow God to speak to your soul. Every day.
- Take one day a week to rest – do little – do less – do things that bless your soul – you know what they are. Every week.
- Take one evening a week to love. If you are married, call it a date night and fight for it with your life, put energy into planning it. If you are not married, spend it with people who build you, who energise you, who bless your soul. Every week.
- Take one weekend a quarter to breathe. Go away – you may be able to afford a weekend away from home, or you may not. Either way, change the rhythm, bolt the doors to your everyday world, and do something different. Every quarter.
- Take one week a year to learn. If you appreciate conferences, do one; if you prefer conversations, have some; if you read, read some. But do it. Every year.
- Take two holidays every year to remember who you are, what is important and why you do what you do. One of these holidays needs to be more than a week – in my experience it takes me three days to change gear. Every year.

My personal history of systematically ignoring this key principle has led to physical illness. Stress that I resolutely denied, shingles and stomach problems that I directly attributed to anything other than overwork and my stubborn inability to let him 'lay me down'. A lack of grace with my staff team when they made understandable mistakes because of my constant weariness and even a lack of joy, at times, with my children who just wanted me to be Dad.

Let him 'lay you down' or you will fall down. And you will let other people down.

Let him lead you

You let him lead you – 'he leads me beside quiet waters' – and stop trying to lead him. After breakfast, Jesus takes Peter aside – perhaps they even walk beside the water – John is following behind (v. 20). Peter allows Jesus to lead, to question him. Peter answers each question, simply and honestly, although it grieves him. This is not the Peter who answers back, who rebuked the Lord for heading to the cross (Matthew 16:22), nor the Peter who protests at Jesus washing his feet (John 13:6, 8), nor the one who confidently claims he will never let Jesus down (John 13:37). Peter allows Jesus to lead him.

Let him restore you

You let him restore you – and you stop striving to learn a new strategy that will get you out of your leadership hole.

Jesus feeds Peter breakfast, they walk and talk, and Jesus confronts Peter with a restoration encounter: 'Do you love me?' Three times he asks and three times Peter answers, 'Yes'. Three times Jesus gives Peter the chance to say the right thing, to reverse his denial, to remind himself who he is.

And with that assurance, he calls him to follow him, he restores him.

Let him watch over you

'I will fear no evil, for you are with me; your rod and your staff, they comfort me.'

Peter's denial was about fear and self-preservation. As he restores him, Jesus tells Peter that he will stay faithful – even through suffering, even through the valley, even through the kind of death he will glorify God with. When you allow the Lord to shepherd you, you stop trying to protect yourself, defend yourself and preserve things and allow him, *Yahweh*

Sabbaoth, God of the angel armies, to do his work in and around your life.

Shepherd Leaders

Shepherding leadership is where I want to leave us, because it's where Jesus leaves us.

Leadership is not just *about* Jesus, it is *for* Jesus. Motive is important here. Why are you even leading? What are you doing it for? In my best moments I answer that question, 'Because I love Jesus.' Why am I serving? Because I love him. But do I? What does the answer to the question, 'Do I love him?' actually look like?

I find it deeply challenging to discover, in this encounter, Jesus suggesting that it looks like 'shepherd'.

Peter eats a hearty breakfast and then Jesus confronts him with a restoration encounter: 'Do you love me?' Three times he asks and three times Peter answers, 'Yes'. Jesus replies by saying, 'Well, shepherd my sheep'. In other words, with me, love is practical and outworked and visible, it is always others-focused. Your leadership vocation is to be a shepherd, in the same way that I am!

Before you and I rush off into an '*I-couldn't-possibly-do-it, I'm-not-Peter, let-alone-Jesus*' pity-fest, realise that a very interesting verbal exchange is taking place. On the first two occasions that Jesus asks the question, he uses *agape* as his word for love. He says, 'Do you *agape,* do you perfect, self-giving love me?' Peter responds with, 'You know that I *phileo* you, I love you as a brother.' On the third occasion Jesus says, 'Do you *phileo* me?'

He asks only for what he knows Peter can give, and then accepts it.

And with that assurance he calls him to shepherd.

'Feed my lambs.'
'Take care of my sheep.'
'Feed my sheep.'

Shepherd. Loving God as a leader always looks like shepherd.

The original Greek word is the word *poimen,* and it has the sense of feeder and protector – someone who is called to care for the entire well-being of the flock. The implication here for us is that our vocation is to shepherd according to our gift and call.

I had the immense privilege of speaking at my father's funeral. He was a well-loved and highly effective shepherd of the flock. At his thanksgiving service I was able to say, as a fitting memorial, 'He loved God and he loved people'. I can't think of a simpler or more wonderful thing to be said of a Jesus-leader. One day, I hope that it will be said of me. Loving God as a Jesus-leader always looks like shepherd.

Please don't hear what I'm not saying. We all have a particular strength in ministry, a 'base' ministry. And that is, in effect, our trade. Our base ministry might be apostolic – pioneering, breaking ground, taking territory. It might be prophetic – hearing from God, for God's people, regarding direction and timing. It might be evangelistic – living out and speaking out good news. It might be pastoral – creating a healthy community of care and interdependence. Or it might be teaching – helping people to grow in the knowledge of God and grow up into the people of God.

We all have different leadership gifts, as the Apostle Paul outlines in Ephesians 4:11, and if we are to see the church of Jesus Christ fulfilling her God-given calling to mission and discipleship, then we need these gifts in balance and tension. We particularly need to rediscover and reframe the apostolic, prophetic and evangelistic gifts – as so often these have been misunderstood and feared, and therefore neglected. But everybody loses out – the Church finds herself unable to break new ground, disabled in hearing from God and with a radical inability to bring people into the kingdom. Those with apostolic, prophetic or evangelistic base ministry gifts find other avenues, outside the local body, to fulfil their calling, which further exacerbates the fears and concerns about the maverick nature of these gifts and further cements the idea that the primary leadership role within the local church is 'pastor-teacher'. Pastors and teachers are vital for the development of the body of Christ, but in a season of falling numbers and declining influence, the church must arrest these trends by embracing the calling and gifting of the apostle, prophet and evangelist, and encouraging them to lead within the church, not just outside it.

Whatever our particular ministry, our vocation as leaders is to shepherd well. Peter was an apostolic leader – his calling was to lead the birth and growth of the early church, to plot its course and to win new people and new territory for this new thing. But his call in this was to shepherd.

I am much more of an apostle-teacher than an evangelist. But my primary call is to shepherd. Leading according to Jesus' model encourages me to grow into a shepherd-apostle, a shepherd-teacher, because my call is to lead the flock. This applies in whatever sphere of leadership you operate and whether you are based in the local church or not.

Your call, if it is Jesus' call, is to shepherd.

Whatever your base ministry – your call is to shepherd

As a pioneer leader, my value to the team does not lie exclusively in my ability to see beyond and take ground. It lies also and vitally in my ability and commitment to take people with me on a journey, to inhabit the land taken. That is at least in part the call of the shepherd.

Where this modelling from the life of Jesus and commissioning in the teaching of Jesus is overlooked or ignored, I believe that two things happen.

1. We implicitly permit every gift outside of '*poimen*' to lack the compassion, mercy and care of the good shepherd.

I am convinced that this was never Jesus' intention. It means that we take territory and lose ground.

2. We relegate the function of shepherding to the pastoral care team and we shrink the role of shepherd in the process.

So what does it look like to shepherd?

Guided guides

Shepherd leaders go ahead and they go with. Shepherds on the hills find a path to the pasture, they know where the cliffs and the bogs are, because they have walked them before. They have fallen off the cliffs and been neck deep in the bogs and guide away from such dangers because they don't want sheep to be hurt or lost. Your experience is your map and your presence is your compass. Your journey as a sheep and your early stumblings as a shepherd are maps for your shepherding adventure. Every path trodden, every cliff fallen off and every bog stuck in are points to guide against on someone else's sheep journey. Rehearse your story well and tell it often.

Your presence is a compass. Maps are only good if you know where you are, which way you are heading. Often your sheep will need a compass for the journey: you are their compass. Your availability to those that you lead is vital. In contrast to much current leadership practice, where the more senior you are, the less available you are, I have discovered that the more experienced you become, the more available you must be, for that is what your experience is for. There are more demands on my time now than ever, but I intentionally make more time to lead by walking around, sharing experience, giving input, getting involved in the leadership lives of my team. For want of another term, 'shepherding them'.

Pope Francis is providing an incredible example of shepherding leadership in our time. He is clearly a humble leader, a man of the people, who understands what it is like to be shepherded. As Pope, part of his responsibility is to set the framework and person description for all of the Catholic church's appointment of Bishops. One of his key filters has been 'I want shepherds who smell of the sheep'.[35] The shepherd leader is not set apart, isolated in his or her office, sending emails, reading Facebook or preparing talks. The shepherd leader prepares by being amongst the people, by interpreting contemporary culture alongside the Scriptures and by forging real friendships, not just virtual ones. The shepherd leader has current, relevant life experience. The shepherd leader is a compass.

Watchful guards

The shepherd leader protects by watching. Shepherds are diligent people, they watch. They watch for the weather, and they watch for predators. Your vocational call involves being discerners of the times and readers of culture. If the sheep you have been given to shepherd are to be warned and protected and grow strong, then you need to know what is happening in the world around and you need to be able to call enemies and have a strong defence against anything that would undermine the health of your sheep.

Shepherds are watchers. You watch TV, news and current affairs programmes. You will not be unaware of what is trending on social media, because this will affect sheep. You will know what is teaching and leading your sheep and how to bring balance and correction. I have found it fascinating and increasingly concerning that we operate and lead in a time where all sheep have multiple leaders. I am not the only leader of my congregation and you are not the only leader of your organisation or your team. The advent of the Internet and the development of blogging and social media, means that those who follow you are very likely following other people. Those who listen to your voice are very likely listening to many other, often conflicting voices. Never has there been more importance for you as a leader in knowing the signs of the times and

[35] *The Catholic Telegraph*, 28 March 2013.

helping those who follow you to navigate themselves through the burgeoning seas of information and opinion. They need you to understand and to help them with filters and tools to read and listen well and interpret and apply well for life.

A prayerful perspective

As a shepherd leader, you will need not only to be present but also to be absent. Not only close to the sheep, but also removed from the sheep. Your perspective is really important, it is your map. Whilst it is vital for you as a shepherd leader to be in the trenches, in the field, on the ground with those you lead, it is also crucial for you to find times to remove yourself, to climb a hill and get a better view, to step aside to think clearly, to remove yourself to pray and get God's perspective. The sheep need a map as much as they need a compass. You and I, as shepherd leaders, have a huge responsibility to plot a path for the journey, to guide through difficult terrain.

I have learned to ask a number of key questions:

1. Where is God leading this community that God has called me to lead? What is the goal?
2. What season are we in? What is the task right now? What should the pace be?
3. What obstacles are we likely to encounter on the way? What strongholds has the enemy set up in our culture? What ways of thinking will we need to deconstruct in order to get to the goal? What are the current, most popular idols in our community that will distract us from the path?
4. Where are the oases, the celebration spots on the map that will get us with joy to the end?

I have discovered that I will never lead the sheep well, unless I climb to a high point and pray, and plot a map.

This posture is just as important and valuable to the sheep as is your presence with them. I have discovered that, whilst those you lead will not always understand why you take time to retreat, why you have a reading week or close your office door, they will understand far less if your organisation withers because you did not have any perspective, any vision, or a bigger plan.

I am convinced that my ability to develop a rhythm and pattern of availability and aloofness combined with my willingness to learn to rest will determine the effectiveness and longevity of the ministry God has called me to. It is that important.

Shepherd-restorers

Peter's journey as a shepherd-leader begins with restoration. I couldn't begin to imagine how many men and women have had their lives turned around by the simple retelling of the story of the fire and the three questions. Peter's vulnerability and willingness to wear with honour the story of failure and restoration has opened the door for many sheep to experience similar grace and healing. Your ability to understand, analyse and articulate brokenness and healing is directly related to your ability to be a shepherd-restorer.

And this is vital if your leadership is to be the leadership of Jesus. Because Jesus is the expert when it comes to restoring broken people and using their superglued-brokenness to minister to brokenness. The church of Jesus Christ must be the gold standard in restoration services. Unfortunately, it so often has been the worst place to get restored.

The shepherd leader develops an ability to restore sheep. The world around us is increasingly becoming a throwaway society; when your car or your kitchen gadget or your vacuum cleaner or your shoes become old and break, you throw them away and buy new ones. We don't 'mend' anymore. Unfortunately, we do the same with people. But God doesn't, and the church mustn't! The written-off, the washed-up and the 'not to be trusted' are often the very stuff that future breakthrough is made of. This is a really difficult and challenging calling, it's messy and fraught with obstacles, it's usually two steps forward and one step back. But it's the ministry of Jesus.

I think some of my strongest, most gifted and able leaders are those who have been divorced, have had terminations, have been restored following pornography addictions or have committed adultery. They have grown into some of the most godly and significant leaders I know.

If you and I are going to lead in Jesus' style, it would be helpful to think through three stages of restoration: a place of forgiveness, a programme of restoration and a process of healing.

A place of forgiveness

In order for restoration to occur, there must be real repentance and real forgiveness. This needs to happen at a moment in time. Remember that the word translated 'repentance' from the Greek is the word *metanoia* which literally means 'to change the way you think'. There must be an understanding of wrong thinking and consequently wrong action in order for there to be sorrow and a rethink. I have never restored to leadership anyone who has not exhibited deep sorrow and regret, not over the fact that they were caught, but over the sin and rebellion and wrong thinking in their life. Never do it, or you will be setting yourself up for failure. I have found that if there is genuine forgiveness at the moment of repentance, that leaves the gate to real restoration wide open.

A programme of restoration

Forgiveness is not, however, the same as restoration. Restoration is a process which takes time. Time to build trust with others, time to build behaviour muscles and ministry habits that will confound a proclivity to destructive activity. You rush restoration at your peril. Often a fall or a fail in leadership comes from an unwillingness to submit to leadership or accountability, and a drift away from community. I would look for and encourage certain stages in the restoration process:

1. A period of active and humble service. It is vital that the one being restored learns to serve again in hidden ways if they are ever going to serve in public ways. Stacking chairs, opening buildings, cleaning floors all test a real desire to be restored.
2. An active desire to seek out genuine accountability. I would look for a regular and vulnerable accountability, self-initiated and regularly entered into as part of the restoration journey.
3. A covenant commitment to a community where there is mutual transparency and where life gets done together.

A process of healing

And there must be healing. This can be a programme of healing that is undergone with help from experts, and with prayer, to make sure that the wound that caused the fall, or the wound caused by the fall, is healed to the extent that it causes no further damage.

Clearly it would be a far easier leadership journey if we never engaged in restoration. We will make mistakes; we will fall again. We will trust people that we should not trust. I have often been tempted to 'throw away and start again'. But I am encouraged to try, because I trust God; I trust that what he has done in healing me and restoring me and transforming me, he can do with anyone. I have spoken harshly, had ungodly ambitions, mistreated people, beaten the sheep when I was called to love them, abused my position, judged harshly and made really bad errors and Father God has not thrown me away. I am also encouraged to try because I trust the community of God. I trust that it is still, despite its well-documented failures, by far the best breeding ground for Jesus-leadership, the best healing ground for broken leaders and the best hothouse for full restoration.

We have a model for this kind of ministry, whether the fall is pre- or post-conversion. The Apostle Paul is totally restored after his encounter with Jesus, and John Mark becomes most useful after being a ministry liability.

The shepherd restores by vulnerability and story but also by discipline and correction. This will not be popular, but it is real. In Psalm 23, the shepherd carries a rod and a staff – a rod to protect and a staff to correct. The staff was used to bring errant sheep back in line and to pull others from the thorns. It is never fun to have to correct those that you lead, but it is just as loving and just as restorative as cooking them breakfast on the beach.

Peter is restored by the great shepherd, with love, to love. By the shepherd, to shepherd.

Jesus finishes his restoration by asking Peter to 'follow me'. All leadership and all restoration to leadership starts here and continues here. Follow Jesus. All leadership that is good leadership is Jesus-leadership.

Peter goes on to lead the church through persecution and into incredible mission. As he nears the end of his leadership journey, he writes his own leadership notes for those who will follow. In 2 Peter 1:3, he tells us we have everything we need to live right with God today. We can know God's unmerited favour in our lives today. We can be at peace with the Creator of this world today. We can lead like Jesus.

Then Peter suggests something that initially appears to be a denial of what has come before, to 'make every effort to add to your faith' (2 Peter 1:5) and he describes leadership virtues: goodness, knowledge, self-control, patience, godliness and brotherly kindness. He calls us to grow in knowledge and perseverance, to develop self-control and exhibit kindness, and he asks us to do so with heroic love – the word translated 'goodness' was used to describe the power of the gods to do heroic deeds. He concludes his list with love not only because he knows that, without it, leadership is a programme or an exercise, but also because he knows that when people look into a community that is led in this way, they will see Jesus.

Whether you ride a quad bike or carry a staff, whether your call is to pioneer or teach, whether the capacity of your leadership is thousands or a few, your vocation is to shepherd for the great shepherd. It's a dirty, hard, noble and heroic calling. A perfect calling. Jesus-leadership is perfect leadership. So lead. Whatever the context, whatever your capacity, wherever you find yourself.

> Lead like Jesus.
> You will change the world.

Trace a circle. Take responsibility. There are no excuses.
Draw a line. Take responsibility. Have no regrets.
Plant a stake. Take responsibility. Let there be no distractions.
And continue to do this, and apprentice others to do this, so that you, and they, might lead like Jesus.